8 Days of Glory

Reflections on Holy Week

LESLIE H. WOODSON

Copyright © 2015 Century House Evangelistic Foundation, Inc.

All rights reserved. No part of this book may be used or reproduced by any means, graphic, electronic, or mechanical, including photocopying, recording, taping or by any information storage retrieval system without the written permission of the publisher except in the case of brief quotations embodied in critical articles and reviews.

First published in 1971 by Beacon Hill Press of Kansas City.
Reprinted 1972 by Baker Book House Company. ISBN 0-8010-9532-8
Reprinted 1994 by Institute for Biblical Excellence (Century House Evangelistic Foundation, Inc.).

WestBow Press books may be ordered through booksellers or by contacting:
WestBow Press
A Division of Thomas Nelson & Zondervan
1663 Liberty Drive
Bloomington, IN 47403
www.westbowpress.com
1 (866) 928-1240

Scripture quotations, unless otherwise noted, are taken from the *New English Bible*, copyright © 1961, 1970 by Cambridge University Press and Oxford University Press. All rights reserved.

Scripture quotations marked "KJV" are taken from the King James Version of the Bible.

Scripture quotations marked "Phillips" are from *The New Testament in Modern English*, J. B. Phillips, copyright 1958. Used by permission of the Macmillan Company.

Scripture quotations contained herein and marked "RSV" are from the *Revised Standard Version of the Holy Bible*, copyright 1946, 1952, 1971 by the Division of Christian Education of the National Council of Churches in the USA. All rights reserved.

Scripture quotations marked "TEV" are from *Today's English Version*, copyright 1966, American Bible Society.

Scripture quotations marked "Moffatt" are from *The Bible: A New Translation*, James Moffatt, copyright 1950, 1952, 1953, 1954 by James A. R. Moffatt. Used by permission of Harper and Row.

Scripture quotations marked "Goodspeed" are from *The New Testament: An American Translation*, Edgar J. Goodspeed, copyright 1923 by the University of Chicago Press.

Because of the dynamic nature of the Internet, any web addresses or links contained in this book may have changed since publication and may no longer be valid. The views expressed in this work are solely those of the author and do not necessarily reflect the views of the publisher, and the publisher hereby disclaims any responsibility for them.

Any people depicted in stock imagery provided by Thinkstock are models, and such images are being used for illustrative purposes only.
Certain stock imagery © Thinkstock.

ISBN: 978-1-4908-6717-5 (sc)
ISBN: 978-1-4908-6718-2 (hc)
ISBN: 978-1-4908-6716-8 (e)
Library of Congress Control Number: 2015901086

Printed in the United States of America.
WestBow Press rev. date: 01/16/2015

To

BETTY

a disciplined helper

a devoted wife

a loving mother

CONTENTS

Foreword ix
Preface xi

SUNDAY
    A Welcome that Made God Cry 1

MONDAY
    A Religion that Made God Angry 13

TUESDAY
    The Day that Made God Tired 23

WEDNESDAY
    And God Rested 37

THURSDAY
    The Day of Suffering Fellowship 51

THURSDAY
    The Night of Divine Sadness 63

THURSDAY
    The Night When the Priests Defied God 75

FRIDAY
    The Morning When the State Deserted God 85

FRIDAY
Mission Accomplished 95
SATURDAY
The Day of Retroactive Atonement 107
SUNDAY
The Day When Death Died 117

Endnotes 129

FOREWORD

When I spoke with Dr. Leslie H. Woodson, I always referred to him as "Pop." He became my second father when I was ten years old. Just a few months ago, Pop died. After months of illness, he was anxious to be with his Savior, the One described in this book. Pop lives even as his Lord lives. The publishing of this book is both a tribute to him by family and friends and a study of importance on the last eight days of Jesus' life. Preachers and Bible teachers return to this book year after year—myself included. It is an excellent study that will guide you through this most important of weeks.

The reality of Pop's faith became more and more evident as he neared death. There was no doubt that he trusted in a resurrected Savior who suffered for him. Pop also modeled faith in suffering. He wrote this book to help you understand better what Jesus did for you. He wanted you to know and love Jesus as he did. Pop had a burden to teach the Bible to as many as possible. His calling fueled his passion for writing. He knew that this would endure. And so it has. May your faith deepen as you work through the events of each of these eight glorious days.

J. D. Shipp
Century House Evangelistic Foundation, Inc.

PREFACE

It has been over a hundred thousand weeks since the death of Christ. One hundred thousand is a lot of just about anything. What is even more astounding and past the ability of most of us to comprehend is the figure of seven hundred thousand, which is approximately the number of days which have elapsed since that time. For the mathematical genius, this represents about seventeen million hours or slightly over a billion minutes. But such figures stagger the imagination, so let's go back to the hundred thousand weeks. To find one week out of all that maze of weeks is a difficult task, to say the least, but there is one single week—or eight days, to be more exact—which merits history's citation as the most spectacular and eternally significant of all.

It began on a Sunday very little different from any other working day. To us, it was a special day set apart from all others; but we have the advantage of the years, and events always look either better or worse in retrospect. The end came on the following Sunday, when all Israel was astir with the strangest news ever heard. We call the first day "Palm Sunday" and the eighth "Easter." Between the humble entrance of a carpenter on Sunday morning and the royal entrance of a King seven days later, Jerusalem and the world were changed.

We have said that this octave in time has been unequaled in importance by any period in history before or since. Indeed, it is unnecessary for any persuasive voice to seek our acceptance of this most obvious truth. During the fifty years which were to follow that momentous week, the apostles and earliest gospel narrators devoted the greater segments of their stories to recounting the proceedings of those eight days Matthew devoted a third of his narrative to the activities of Holy Week; Mark and Luke, 40 percent each; and John, slightly more. The average space devoted by the four Evangelists to this period is in excess of 35 percent. Martin Kahler has suggested that the Evangelists have written accounts of the Passion with introductions. To them, and to the early church, there was no question about the importance of the last week in Jesus' earthly life.

World history's watershed stands squarely in the center of the Incarnation, but the birth of Christ would have resulted in little more than the birth of any other religious leader if there had been no cross and no empty tomb. In a real sense, the entire life of Jesus was only one event in three acts, the acts being clearly discernible in birth to baptism, baptism to crucifixion, and crucifixion to ascension. Each act included its particular scenes. All of these events in the thirty-three years of Christ's earthly pilgrimage are only facets of the many-sided and all-inclusive act of divine redemption. It was during these final days, however, that the budding flower, to all eyes crushed beyond repair, burst into full and glorious bloom.

Books and articles about the last week of Jesus' life are written by the volumes. There always seems to be something new to be said, and, even if it is not so new, it needs to be said again and again. Many publishing concerns bring out a new work by some distinguished scholar or warm-hearted pastor each spring in preparation for the penitent season of Lent. Thousands of clergy return every year to preach on the theme, which never grows old. And, though most of the activities outside the church building are of a purely secular nature, for at least a week every year the public is reminded that the events which transpired during Holy Week more than two thousand years ago are still worth celebrating.

It is significant to note that, while skeptics of the final efficacy of the work of Christ are free with their accusations, we have yet to hear of one who has an alternate plan for salvation. Had God known any better way, any less drastic method, for the redemption of humankind than the cross and vacated burial vault, it is reasonable to assume that He would have used it. In view of the fact that deliverance from the curse of evil has come to the world by the events of that week, we are wise to dig and sift once again in that rich soil for traces of shining gold dust which have been overlooked by others prospecting before us. Anyone who believes that the veins have been exhausted is in for an exciting surprise.

Attempts to rationalize away the blunt views held by witnesses of the actual events and by writers of the New Testament and early church have been so wildly manufactured by clever minds as to be a dime a dozen. What is needed today is a sane and reverent analysis of the major occurrences that took place during those eight days, a contemporary approach that does not alter the content of those sacred and eternally significant days of glory. God was at work in Jesus Christ in a unique and climactic way, one which has never been repeated because what happened was a once-and-for-all event. All the hopes and dreams of man converge on that one solitary week. The past, present, and future are understandable only as they are related to those days.

All history hinges on that divine act by which God was and is "reconciling the world unto himself" (2 Cor. 5:19).

With the increasing pre-Reformation emphasis on salvation by works that is making the rounds in theological whirlpools and local church circles of late, someone needs to sound the Pauline and Lutheran mandate that man is still saved by what God has done, not by works, regardless of how meritorious they may be. Christianity is becoming identified with the redemption of social structures by man. Indeed, something needs to be done about social evils, and the Church of Jesus Christ ought to do it; but mankind will not find salvation in any man-made utopia of justice and equality, good as that would be. People cannot save themselves. We should know that by now. Salvation is still essentially involved with what God has done in Christ during those eight days of glory.

In almost every instance, the discussion of Holy Week revolves around seven days. The week, which begins and ends on Sunday, actually comprises eight days. The usual pattern is to present a critique of the activities of each day, with the exception of Saturday. The Sabbath, however, is seldom even mentioned in Lenten studies concerned with the last week. This is probably due to the widely divergent views that have been taken by scholars who are willing to give time to the enigma of a living God in a grave. This neglected day will be given fair treatment in this book, for it is the author's firm conviction that no day was more engaging for the Master than that day when His earthly ministry was transferred to a new dimension.

The number seven was, in earliest days in Israel, the symbol for perfection and completion. There were seven days of creation, the seventh year, and seven planets. The entire universe was believed to be built on the number seven. As time passed, people began to exalt the number eight, since the sum of the seven figures was an eighth, the totaling figure thus symbolizing completion even better than the earlier seven. Gradually, the digit eight replaced the seven as the number of perfection. The last week of Jesus' earthly life was a completely perfect one, for it embraced eight, not seven, days. Easter Sunday was the first day of the week, it is true, but it also came to be known as the eighth day and symbolized the unity of the seven, the tying together of the events of Sunday through Saturday, and a new beginning for Christ and the whole world. The eighth day was both an end and a beginning, the end of the bondage to law and the beginning of freedom in grace. For this reason, I have chosen to call that Easter Sunday, plus the seven days which led to it, "eight days of glory." As we think together, we will hopefully see why this is so.

—Leslie H. Woodson

SUNDAY

When he came in sight of the city, he wept over it. (Luke 19:41)[1]

A Welcome that Made God Cry

It all began early one morning when Jesus commanded two of His disciples to go into the village of Bethphage (though the narrators are not quite clear as to whether the town was Bethphage or Bethany) on a mission to find a young burro. Most likely, in view of the strange things that He had been saying and doing during the last few days, there would have been some puzzlement about the purpose of the errand. The Master had never been known to ride on anything before. He must have covered hundreds of miles on foot, but not once could they remember His having been transported anywhere by any other method except when He crossed a lake in a boat. However, if they wondered why the Lord was making such a request, the disciples made no mention of it.

The Lord provided careful details as to how the burro should be found and procured. Quite obviously, the owner was a friend of the Lord and, on some earlier occasion, had agreed to allow Him the use of his little donkey. The answer that the dispatched pair were told to give to any inquisitive skeptic was, "Our Master needs it, and will send it back here without delay." It would appear that this was a kind of password that had been acceptable to both the owner and his servants. How long in advance our Lord knew He was going to make His final entry into Jerusalem in this dramatic manner is not possible to speculate. Unquestionably, the whole situation had been brewing for a long time, and He was waiting for the proper moment, the occasion of the Passover, to carry out His plans.

It may be safely assumed that this act of entry into Jerusalem was one of the most difficult moves ever made by the Son of God. In time of war, kings rode upon prancing stallions, but the ass was chosen as a royal vehicle in periods of peace. In His choice to ride at all, Jesus was proclaiming himself as King. There was the chance that the people would finally recognize His true mission by this symbolic act, but it was a slim hope. Such an entry might result in laughter by people viewing Him as a spectacle of lunacy. It might also anger those who would think of Him as making a jest of the role of the long-awaited Messiah. And there was the risk that the people would rally to acclaim Him as the kind of king He could not be—a theocratic conqueror who would bless a nation without its repenting. The outcome was hidden, but it was a chance that Christ felt He had to take.

Such a confrontation, what with the messianic fervor so thick in the air at festival time, was bound to be dangerous. Jesus knew well that He would probably get into serious trouble, regardless of how the populace responded to the drama being enacted before them. But He "set his face resolutely towards Jerusalem" (Luke 9:51). And by this time, the cross loomed large on the horizon for Christ, like some hungry monster waiting to consume Him. From the very beginning, His life had been one long day of trouble. It was true that throngs of people waited on His ministry with absorbing minds, but everywhere He looked, there was trouble lurking in the shadows. What He had feared from the very first was about to develop into a gory end for the much too short life of God's Son.

John relates how the news raced ahead as Christ descended the Mount of Olives: "Lazarus has been raised from the dead! The day of the Messiah is here! Prepare to meet Him!" With that exciting news, the people, who were already intoxicated with the festive air, raised their voices in loud cries of joyous anticipation. Before Christ ever came in sight of the city streets, which were lined with thousands of happy pilgrims, shouts of "hosanna" could be heard. The enthusiasm of the disciples, joined with the wildly extravagant gestures of the waiting crowds on the outskirts of Jerusalem, grew into a massive wave of ear-deafening uproars. For the people, it was a time to rejoice. This day was the Epiphany of the long-awaited King of Israel. To remain quiet would have been treason to the welcoming throngs.

This is not to say that everybody was jubilant to see the entering Messiah. There were numbers of men and women in the crowd to whom Jesus had given healing, recovery of sight, deliverance from demons, and simple love and compassion. These people were overjoyed to see the accolades being given to Him. But there were others whose traditions the Master had trampled under His feet. These people shouted, too, but their words, drowned out in the din of confusion, were angry invectives and snarling curses. Jesus, however, was conscious of this element, which would help to create the conditions for the crucifixion within the week. He was also aware that many of those who were shouting most loudly for His enthronement would be soon shouting for His entombment or sitting idly by, indifferent as to the final outcome.

Not even the Twelve understood the significance of what was taking place. Judas Iscariot was doing his best to incite those who stood at the edge of the crowd and were slow to join in the cheering until they understood more about what was happening. He had already made some definite plans to give impetus to the mounting desire to crown Christ as King. Simon the Zealot was right at home in the array of colorfully robed, ardent advocates of political freedom. Philip was a little dumfounded by the whole thing, just as he had always been in the wake of everything that happened. Nathanael was somewhat skeptical of any such sudden eruption of support that did not have the undergirding of scholarly thought and planning. He was afraid that the support would die as quickly as it had been born.

Peter, James, and John were enjoying the attention being given to their Master. With a wary eye for any trace of trouble, Peter kept his hand on the sword that he had tucked in his girdle. After three years, not one of the Twelve had grasped the complete identity of Christ or the purpose for which He had come into the world. "With all His explanations, it was not until the Fiftieth Day that they came at last to the full comprehension of His enthronement as Lord and saw that the Cross belonged in His career as King."[2]

Suddenly, the beast on which Jesus was riding stopped. People bumped into one another because there had been no warning that there would be a pause in the journey. No one knew why the caravan had come to a halt, and many far back in the crowd were calling out for the party to move ahead. Those nearest the Lord, however, noted that something was wrong with the King on the burro. His shoulders were shaking vigorously as though He were laughing. It would have been in order, because all the others were beside themselves with joy. But, if He were laughing, there was no hint of it on His face. Deep furrows had formed in His brow as He sat staring pitifully at the city that stretched before Him. He was weeping! Tears were running down His cheeks as the deep fountains in His soul welled up and rushed out through His eyes.

There were numerous times when Jesus was deeply moved by conditions that prevailed around Him, but there are only two recorded instances of His having wept. The first was on the occasion of the death of Lazarus, His dear friend, whose sisters were overwhelmed with grief. Arriving at the tomb and feeling deeply the intense agony of bereavement that had gripped Lazarus' family and friends, the Lord gave expression to His deepest emotions and joined Mary and Martha in their crying. It is a lovely picture of the way in which God enters with us into our helplessness and despair. Goethe, the famous German writer of the late 1700s and early 1800s, confesses in his autobiography that he lost the ability to weep as he grew older. Many of us are like that. We become hardened and calloused to the tragedies of human existence. But not our Lord. The occasions of His crying were near the end of His journey, when He was quite mature and yet tender.

Only one other instance of weeping in the life of our Lord is known to us. It was not in Gethsemane or on the cross, where men were expected to weep and curse, nor was it when His trusted disciples betrayed and denied Him. He never wept for Himself and even asked the women who lined the Via Dolorosa as He climbed to the place of execution, "Do not weep for me; no, weep for yourselves and your children" (Luke 23:28). He was too much a man to weep for Himself or desire sympathy from anyone else. In both incidents where Christ is said to have cried, He wept for others. The second occasion of His weeping was on Sunday evening of the Holy Week when He came in sight of the city.

The tears ran down His cheeks precisely because He had witnessed nothing but blind jubilation as He rode into the Holy City. He lamented, "If only you had known, on this great day, the way that leads to peace" (Luke 19:42)! But alas, the people "did not recognize God's moment when it came."

There is a real sense in which it is historically true that the big step, one in a whole series of blind acts of bigotry and pride that precipitated the conditions for the final undoing of Israel, was the fanatically blind act of missing the whole meaning of Palm Sunday, God's last dramatic call to repentance.

> Whenever we see a civilization go down in ruin because some main feature of its life is at variance with the principles of Christ, there we see Christ coming in Judgment and exercising that authority which is given to Him in heaven and on earth.[3]

Had the nation recognized the lowly man approaching on a lowly beast as their God of peace and love, they would have dressed in sackcloth and put ashes on their heads rather than wave palm branches.

It has been said that the sorrowful Savior wept for the dead at the graveside of Lazarus and for the living at the gate of the city. On the surface, this is true. In a more realistic way, Christ may be said to have been weeping for the living when He wept for Mary and Martha. It was for them, for their deep grief, that

His tears flowed. It was not at the graveside of Lazarus, but at the graveside of Israel, that He wept for the dead. It was a deep spiritual death which had produced complete and irrevocable numbness to the Life when He appeared in their midst. Lazarus had responded to the call to life, but Israel had refused its day of resurrection. The chill of death was everywhere. The priests and people, going through their Passover ritual in routine fashion, were like ghostly apparitions from the shades of Sheol.

The palms were symbols of victory, in conflict with a distinct flavor of war. They had been used at the Feast of Tabernacles when Judas Maccabeus had recovered the holy temple from the Syrians (2 Macc. 10:7). Thus, it was not likely that any Jew could see the palm branch without seeing political reflections and mental images of military conquest. With little doubt, the use of the palms, accompanied by the shouts of pure political messianism, was an indication that they had missed the whole purpose in Christ's entry into Jerusalem. They really expected Him to continue the old fight, only on a grander scale.

Jesus knew that it would be futile to think of taking arms against the might of Rome. This is what He meant when He spoke through His tears. "Your enemies will set up siege-works against you; they will encircle you and hem you in at every point; they will bring you to the ground, you and your children within your walls, and not leave you one stone standing on another" (Luke 19:43–44). There was not a chance in the world that their stubborn policies of hate and pride would work. No wonder He asked the women to add their tears to His in lamenting the fall of the nation!

He had come to show them "a more excellent way" (1 Cor. 12:31 KJV). It was the way of love. Much earlier, He had said what seemed to everyone to be a wildly extravagant statement.

> Love your enemies; do good to those who hate you; bless those who curse you; pray for those who treat you spitefully. When a man hits you on the cheek, offer him the other cheek too; when a man takes your coat, let him have your shirt as well. (Luke 6:27–29)

Surely, He did not have Rome in mind. If He did, reasoned the multitudes, then He was a raving lunatic! But, He did have Rome in mind, as well as all peoples whom we often despise for what they have done, or seem to have done, to us. While Israel was under the power of Rome, it was granted special privileges and given the advantage of many Roman boons. It could have been far worse, and it would be if somebody did not learn to love his enemy. After all, it was to be Israel's chance, as well as its duty, to bring Rome to God.

Jesus wept because of the desolation that was to come to a people whom God loved and called His own. He wept because the future was ominous with clouds of war and judgment. He wept because the people of God had blown their last chance to bless all nations with the covenant of loving forgiveness. He wept because His people would soon see their nation collapse. He wept because not even God could change the clamor for political messianism into a desire for a spiritual reign of truth and love. There was no chance that the people would receive Him as Savior. A king who sanctioned their proud rebellion was all they wanted.

What a contrast! Among the splendors of the city in the darkening rays of the evening sun, there stood, silhouetted against the horizon, the tall and stately towers of the temple of Herod, which dominated the most sacred rock in the world—the place where Abraham had gone to sacrifice Isaac. But superimposed upon the beauty of the ancient city, like a filmy death shroud, was the Jerusalem which the Master envisioned. The Enemy was hovering over the sacred streets, cries of battle rent the air, and the walls had already begun to topple. As the vision widened, every stone was hurled to the ground. Blood ran down the crevices in the rocks, and here and there truncated limbs and decapitated bodies lay scattered across the debris as food for scavenger beasts. Multitudes shut within the walls of the city died of starvation while Titus waited for surrender. Over a million men perished, and nearly a hundred thousand were carried into captivity, where they died in the amphitheaters of Caesarea and Antioch or in the slave mines of Sinai.

God had been good to Israel. In spite of its continual rebellion, its lapses into idolatry, and its failure to carry out its mission to the Gentiles, the God of the covenant had been patient and slow to wrath. But not even God's patience is inexhaustible! The days of glory were running out, and judgment was in the air.

> Now, other days would come; not days of peace, but days of the sword. Jesus foresaw the times of Nebuchadnezzar returning, the times of Pompey and Varus. He would go the way of His passion, but He could no longer avert disaster from Jerusalem.[4]

Matthew records a saying of Jesus which is similar to the lament which fell from His lips as He caught sight of the gleaming, city.

> O Jerusalem, Jerusalem, the city that murders the prophets and stones the messengers sent to her! How often have I longed to gather your

children, as a hen gathers her brood under her wings; but you would not let me. Look, look! there is your temple, forsaken by God. And I tell you, you shall never see me until the time when you say, "Blessings on him who comes in the name of the Lord." (Matt. 23:37–39)

Luke includes these identical words in his narrative (13:34–35), but inserts them in a series of encounters with the people which took place earlier in the ministry of Jesus. Matthew remembers them as having been uttered during Holy Week. It is probably true that this warning was often upon the lips of the Master and that both Matthew and Luke are correct. The one thing which brought tears to the eyes of Christ and unbearable pain to His heart was the obtuse numbness with which the people of God faced their destiny.

We do not fully sense the traumatic upheaval that broke upon the Savior as He beheld the city unless we note the word which Luke uses for *wept*. It is not *edakrusen*, which implies quiet and reserved weeping, the kind of crying which one muffles with a handkerchief. That was the word employed to describe the quiet weeping of Jesus at the grave of Lazarus. But here, Luke uses a much different word, *eklausen*, which means loud lamentation and deep wailing, the kind of weeping that literally shakes a person to pieces when in the grip of inexpressible anguish.

What Jesus saw and felt as He gazed on that beautiful city, on the first day of Holy Week, was enough to shake the Son of God to the depths of His divine being. The spirit of our Lord was keenly perceptive and sensitive to the plight of His people. He had compassion for them when they were in need, was filled with indignation when He saw their self-righteousness, breathed loving forgiveness when they recognized their sin, and broke down under the weight of their blind rebellion.

If people had only opened their eyes, only recognized God when He visited them in Jesus Christ, it could have been so different. The Lord had used every means known to Him to reveal His true identity and mission without involving the nation in charges of subversive reaction against Rome. How could He make the nation see that His was not a kingdom built on force, that His reign among men had nothing to do with Caesar's throne or the imperial household?

How could He best go about the Father's business of making people aware of the presence of God in their midst, of creating a people of love and forgiveness? How to bring people to the foot of the throne of God, where they would find forgiveness for their own sin and an attitude of forgiveness toward their enemies, who were also guilty before God? It was not easy. He knew that. In fact, on Palm Sunday, it was finally clear that there was nothing He could say or do that would cause them to recognize God. "He came unto his own, and his own received him not," because, as John puts it, "they knew him not" (John 1:10–11 KJV). Indeed, He was "the stranger of Galilee." And that broke His heart.

> He alone was silent and sad among this excited multitude, the marks of the tears He had wept over Jerusalem still on His cheek ... He spake not, but only looked around about upon all things, as if to view the field on which He was to suffer and die. And now the shadows of evening were creeping up; and, weary and sad, He once more returned with the twelve disciples to the shelter and rest of Bethany.[5]

MONDAY

My house will be called a house of prayer for all peoples. But you have turned it into a hideout for thieves. (Mark 11:17 TEV)[1]

A Religion that Made God Angry

Only Matthew and Mark record the episode surrounding Jesus' failure to find any fruit on a pretentious fig tree at which He hoped to be able to break His night-fast. John does not mention the instance, and neither does Luke, unless the parable that is related much earlier in the third narrative (Luke 13:6–9) is a version of this same event. After the night of rest—and it is probable that Jesus slept little after the disappointment of the previous day—the Lord commenced His return journey to Jerusalem, fully intent on creating dramatic situations of judgment that could not be misread by even the dullest Jew. When he found a fig tree without fruit, nature had provided him with a ready-made object lesson for the disciples.

Although "it was not the season for figs," the tree was in full leaf. It is a known fact that the Palestinian fig tree bears its fruit before producing its foliage. The presence of leaves was recognized as a definite sign of figs. When Jesus approached the tree, however, and pushed aside the leaves, there was not a single fig to be found. He exclaimed, "May no one ever again eat fruit from you" (Mark 11:14). This was not the remark of a peeved child who, unable to get what he wants when he wants it, throws an ugly temper fit. The Lord was not angry with the tree, but He was indignant with a nation which He found to be perfectly symbolized by the tree. As Farrar, in his inimitable way, puts it, "The sap was circulating; the leaves made a fair show; but of fruit there was none. Fit emblem of a hypocrite, whose external semblance is a delusion and a sham—fit emblem of the nation in whom the ostentatious profession of religion brought forth no fruit of good living—the tree was barren."[2]

There are some who accuse Jesus of acting in a manner unbecoming to a holy prophet. He is said to be "throwing his weight around," pronouncing judgment on an unconscious tree out of a sense of personal injury. This is not so. John the Baptist had said, three years earlier, "Already the axe is laid to the roots of the trees; and every tree that fails to produce good fruit is cut down and thrown on the fire" (Matt. 3:10). Luke recalls Jesus' having told a parable to enforce the truth of the Baptist's word of violent judgment.

Now, at the end of His preaching ministry, the Lord is using the most powerful form of teaching available—the dramatic medium of didactic influence which leaves its indelible impression upon the mind through the window of the eye. The disciples might forget what John and He had said, but they would not be apt to forget soon what they were about to see happen to the fig tree. The next morning, Peter called attention to the desiccated tree, which stood before them as a warning against hypocrisy and impenitence.

Having found no fruit on the precocious fig tree, Jesus was strengthened in His resolve to proceed to the temple and confront the deceived multitudes with the true nature of worship, in contrast to that which the priests were endorsing. With predetermined resolution, the Master walked briskly up the temple steps and into the large court where travelers from afar were bargaining with the sellers of sacrificial birds and animals for a specimen worthy of the Passover. These sacrifices could have been purchased much more cheaply in the marketplaces, but the priests usually found blemishes in such lambs and doves, which rendered them unacceptable. Outside the temple, a pair of pigeons could be obtained for as little as sixty-five cents. Inside the sacred precincts the charge was in excess of two dollars! This was a convenient and nefarious way for the priests to line their own pockets. It is no wonder that the Lord, sensitive to this prostitution of the sacrificial system, described the Jewish authorities behind the traffic in the temple as "a den of robbers."

As if it were not enough that the people should be fleeced in the purchasing their sacrificial animals, it is also true that the priests had set up money changers' tables, where a charge was made to convert the travelers' money into the shekels of the sanctuary. Currencies, normally carried about by foreign pilgrims at the Passover, were not acceptable for paying a debt to God. Neither the Roman denarii nor the Attic drachmas were permitted because of the pagan portraits stamped upon them. To get his money exchanged, a poor Jew often paid as much as he earned for a full day's work. The exploitation of the poor in the name of religion is an ever recurring practice in church history.

Martin Luther was reacting in the sixteenth century against the very abuse that our Lord deplored in Jewry.

John places this incident at the beginning of Jesus' ministry, after the miracle at Cana in Galilee (2:13–22). Some scholars such as Edersheim and Farrar take this to mean that this messianic act was performed twice, once at the outset of our Lord's ministry for warning, and again at the conclusion for judgment. The fact that John does not mention the incident in the proceedings of the last week and that the other narrators fail to include it any earlier reflects the idea that John was not interested in writing a chronological history but only in the facets of Jesus' life which threw light on His deity. The authorities would not have been so surprised—possibly, they would have been on guard—had the self-acclaimed teacher from Nazareth scourged the temple before. Be that as it may, the cleansing of the temple fits in here and was another reason for the mounting bitterness that led the Master to the brow of Golgotha.

Some significance may be attached to the interesting observation that it is John only who mentions the "whip of cords." Each of the other three narrators uses the verb for *drive*, which certainly suggests force, but John does not employ any term describing how the word of Jesus was enforced. No sticks or rods were allowed in the temple, and it is probable that the cords mentioned were rushes used for animal bedding. Those who object to the use of force by a God of love should remember that the one disciple most deeply loving was the one who did not fear to mention the use of a whip. Genuine love always has judgment in it, and, while we may rightly assume that the whip was not laid upon the men themselves, the sight of a whip may have reminded the greedy priests that God's judgment would have real sting in it!

The actual use of the whip was not necessary at all. "It is said that He overthrew the tables of the money-changers, and the seats of the sellers of doves, but there is no suggestion that He laid hands on the money-changers and the traders."[3] It was enough that these vendors should see the fiery indignation in His eyes, see the firm set of His face, and hear the demanding tone of His voice. No justification is to be found for explaining away this incident on the basis of the use of force, dramatically symbolized in a whip of cords, by a God of love. There is a stormy north side to the character of Jesus.

Of course, there is a clearly discernible reason why the money changers did not resist this violent act of the untutored Galilean. Nothing is so weak as a conscience filled with guilt. And there is every evidence that these temple hucksters and priests knew that they were engaged in something very wrong. Sin is never a source of strength. Vice can never hold its own for long before invincible virtue. In their hearts, these temple profaners knew that the angry young Nazarene was right and that He was doing only what churchmen should have had the courage to do long ago. People who stand firmly against the misuse of a place of prayer and worship are usually despised and rejected, but in our saner moments we all know that they are right.

What was it that so incensed the Master as He stood in the midst of the obfuscating atmosphere of religion that He found in the temple? The exploitation of pilgrims from afar by using the holy hill of Zion as a marketplace was bad enough, but there was something much more serious than even this. As the temple was desecrated by the presence of avaricious priests, the dung and stench of animals, and the hucksters' shouts of victims for sale, there was little chance that anyone would be able to worship. The whole sickening affair was located in the court of the Gentiles, and, in view of the Jews' disdain for pagans, the priests may have excused such practice as long as it remained within that area. But that is just the point.

At the beginning of the covenant relationship with Abraham, God had made it perfectly clear that the only reason for His choice of the Hebrews was that they might minister in love to the pagans. "In thee shall all families of the earth be blessed" (Gen.12:3). Later, when Solomon built the temple, it was made clear that the Gentiles were to be given access to a place of prayer. From days of old, it had been understood that the mission of the Hebrew people was the evangelism of the heathen cultures which subsisted around them. Jesus quotes, as a reason for His zealous concern that the temple be used for its divinely instituted purpose, from Jeremiah's word of judgment (7:11) upon the wicked nation of the sixth century BC, "My house shall be called a house of prayer for all the nations. But you have made it a robbers' cave" (Mark 11:17).

There was no other place where the Gentiles could worship except in this outer court specially designed for them. Without question, the Master despised the segregation of the house of God into specific quarters for Gentiles, Jewish women, Israelites, and priests. The secularization taking place in the court of the Gentiles was no worse than the segregation that had become a way of life for the Hebrew people. If the pagans were not to be allowed beyond a designated barrier, and if the area reserved for their search after God were filled with cacophony and marketing enterprises, then how could Israel ever expect to reach the outsider with the message of God?

The breaking down of "the middle-wall of partition," about which Paul was so concerned, had begun already with Jesus many years before. When He healed the Syro-Phoenician woman's daughter and welcomed the Greeks, the wall received its first undermining crack. While the early church at the Council of Jerusalem (Acts 15) commenced the work of removing the dividing wall, the blow that weakened its foundations had been struck much earlier in the temple on Monday of Holy Week.

What the Jew knew in his heart but tried to forget in his heated nationalism was that the religion embraced by the chosen people was to be an inclusive faith. It was never intended to exclude anybody who honestly sought God. What Jesus was saying that day in the temple was not new. It was a protest against the profaning of God's house which had been considered a heinous evil since the first days of the original temple built during the reign of Solomon. The way in which He did it was new indeed, for He literally exploded a bombshell in the middle of a complacent church. And there are people in every congregation who feel that a pastor or layperson who dares to do anything constructive without going through the proper channels and committees is to be anathema!

If the action of the Lord is to be thought of as explosive, then the statement recorded by John was just as shattering. "Destroy this temple," said Jesus, "and in three days I will raise it again" (John 2:19). John explains that the temple to which He referred was His body, but the Jews did not so understand His statement and used it as evidence against Him at His trial. It is possible that Jesus may have actually been referring to both. Clearly, what was going on in the court of the Gentiles was a destructive act that would bring upon the Romans an utter chaos. The temple, once destroyed, would be replaced by the Son of God with a true temple in which the Spirit of God would dwell. This could have been a reference to His resurrection (the body being considered the repository, or temple of Jehovah) or to the building of the Christian Church, whose initial foundation was laid at Pentecost. Indeed, the new Israel[4] would no longer need the profaned temple but would stand in a new covenant relationship with God, which would render them the temple of God themselves. Wherever they were to meet together, there would be the true temple.

Brown accepts this explanation, which makes Jesus' words refer to the actual temple rather than His body, when he writes, "If they do destroy the Temple, Jesus claims that He will replace it shortly with the messianic Temple of unspecified nature."[5] Edersheim, on the other hand, strongly emphasizes in a footnote of his prodigious work, "I cannot see in the words of Jesus any direct reference to the abrogation of the material Temple and its services, and the substitution of the Church for it. Of course, such was the case, and implied in His Crucifixion and Resurrection, though not alluded to here."[6] Perhaps the entire discussion is of such an academic nature as to warrant no more than this passing note.

No sooner had the Master performed His act and made His explanation than "the chief priests and the doctors of the law heard of this and sought some means of making away with him" (Mark 11:18). Mark infers that one reason for this consultation of demonic forces in clerical garb was because the churchmen were afraid of Jesus' uncanny ability to cast a spell over the people and also of His unknown source of power for forcing issues and demanding redress of wrongs. The natural tendency, when we are afraid of something which challenges us, is to try to destroy it. The Master was actually threatening the position and prestige of the religious leaders, and, unless He was stopped, the whole system of ceremonial and sacrificial religion for which they stood was destined for disaster.

From the earliest words and deeds of the Galilean ministry, Jesus was "digging His own grave." The more He said, the more determined were the churchmen to dispose of the troublesome meddler. Most scholars agree that it was the raising of Lazarus that sparked the welcome on Palm Sunday, and the final decision of the council that the popular teacher of a false religion must be liquidated before the end of the Passover. Obviously, the pretender on a burro had accepted the praise of the masses, who thought of Him as some kind of Messiah. False messiahs had been around before and had been taken care of in due time. But no one had ever had the audacity to do what Jesus of Nazareth was doing. Having accepted the accolades of the people, He now upset the practices of the temple at the holiest time of the year. Something had to be done immediately.

With shades of coming darkness moving into the many-columned precincts of the temple, the weary and spent rabbi took His twelve followers and began the trek back to Bethany, where they were staying until Thursday night and from which they would commute to Jerusalem. Rest was what He needed most at the moment, and there was no place where safety from the priests and the people could be better found than at the home of Lazarus, whom He had raised from the dead only a week before. In the company of friends, the Lord would find relaxation and encouragement for the morrow. But only in the solitude of the night, in the wee hours of the morning, was He to find the strength He needed to face the animosity and vengeance of religious fanatics who were out to get Him.

TUESDAY

You call yourselves leaders, and yet you can't see an inch before your noses, for you filter out the mosquito and swallow the camel. (Matt. 23:24 Phillips)[1]

The Day that Made God Tired

Tuesday of Holy Week was an unusually busy and rigorously demanding day for the Son of Man. It was His last day of public ministry, and He crammed as much into it as possible. In his scriptural outline of this history-making week, Bundy lists fifteen incidents as having taken place on this third day.[2] The day began with Simon Peter's calling attention to the fig tree, which had withered during the night. We have already discussed this in the preceding chapter. As had been the case with both Sunday and Monday, so also with Tuesday: The day concluded with the return of Jesus to His lodging outside the city. Sandwiched between these two acts was enough activity to tire even the mythical Hercules.

Both Matthew and Mark make the teaching on the power of

prayer a lesson drawn from the withering fig tree. Luke includes it within the context of this same day but says nothing about the tree. It will be remembered that the third Evangelist records an earlier parabolic teaching that may be a version of this same event. Matthew, however, has the Master impart an almost identical lesson (17:19-20) following the exorcising of a demon at the foot of the Mount of Transfiguration. This variation in chronology may again indicate that Jesus, as any good teacher, used repetition to get His message imbedded in the thought of His disciples. Growing out of the whole incident was an observation about faith and prayer, so natural to the event as to be too good to overlook.

No sooner had the Master, with His motley group of confused disciples, entered the city than the scribes and elders accosted Him with a question about His authority for doing "these things." Nothing is said which would clarify the meaning of the things to which they were making reference, but it is almost certain that the inquiry was an angry demand to know why He had acted so violently while in the temple the day before. Who did this untutored and youthful upstart think He was, anyway, challenging the long-established and accepted customs of the Hebrew nation?

The priests and rabbis knew exactly where they had gotten their authority to officiate in the temple. It had come from the ordained hierarchy, but this carpenter from Nazareth was clearly an impostor. He had not been to any rabbinical school, nor had He been granted authorization by the proper church officials to interfere in the practice of religion. There had been no *Semikhah* (ordination), which was required for anyone who wished to "teach" with authority. There was no possible way in which He could defend Himself against the charge of "operating without a license." Indeed, the council had undoubtedly met during the night and agreed to confront the obnoxious young prophet with a series of questions designed to impale the Lord on the horns of a dilemma and embarrass Him in the presence of the people.

In His inimitable manner of disputation, Jesus turned the question into a surprise move by countering with an inquiry of His own. "The baptism of John," asked Christ, "was it from heaven, or of men?" While the multitudes did undergo John's baptism of repentance, it had never been sanctioned in established circles as being valid. The question was the kind of counterpunch that leaves one's opponent so off-balance that he cannot manage another thrust of his weapon.

Bearing in mind the strong feelings of the people who believed John to have been a prophet, it would have been most unwise to publicly express doubt about the origin of the Baptist's ministry. Therefore, though the priests desired to speak plainly regarding their disdain for the last of the prophets, there remained only one safe response—that of acknowledging his baptism as legitimate. This, however, they dared not do, since Jesus would have been certain to question their refusal to recognize the validity of John's work. Either way they chose, their answer would have incriminated them and placed them in the exact spot into which they had hoped to force the Lord.

Consider what they finally replied: "We cannot tell." What the churchmen really meant was, "We dare not tell!" They could not afford to antagonize the people or give points to their declared enemy. Jesus, knowing that the interrogation was planned to ensnare Him, freed Himself from being embroiled in a useless wrangle on the basis that no debate can ever be of value if one side refuses to answer questions. It should be noted that Christ did not suggest, as had the priests and elders, that He was unable to provide the information requested, but rather that He would not do so unless His enemies were willing to be honest.

Let no one imagine that the Son of God did not know who He was or from whence He had come. It has been argued that the Lord had no messianic consciousness but that the early church read this consciousness into its hero after the resurrection. Canon Liddon rightly declared,

> He distinctly places Himself on terms of equality with the Father, by a double claim. He claims a parity of working power, and He claims an equal right to the homage of mankind ... How fearful is such a claim if the Son be only human; how natural, how moderate, how just, if He is in very deed Divine!"[3]

Poignantly aware of His true identity, Jesus Christ was also keenly conscious of His right to refuse involvement in any prolonged situation that would accomplish no goal for God, the purpose behind the contention being one of blind, bigoted hatred.

Defeated in their endeavor to get Him in trouble with ecclesiastical powers, the priests revamped their strategy so as to bring Jesus into conflict with civil authorities. Personal grievances are set aside in the emergency which arises when energies must be combined to combat a common enemy. Thus it was on this day when the Pharisees joined with their sworn enemy, the Herodians. Together, they sought out the political, social, and religious threat personified in Jesus and began their cross-examination.

Behind all their drooling flattery was the hateful intent itself.

"We are sure, Master, that you are courageous and brilliant and sincere," they commenced. It seemed like good psychology for getting what one wanted, but amateur psychologists should never try to pull their wisdom on the Master himself! Thinking that He was so "sweet-talked" as to be clay in their hands, they continued, "Is it lawful to pay taxes to Caesar or not?" So that was the catch!

The cunning plot was to pin the Master between a yes, which would have made the multitude skeptical of His messiahship, or a no, which was certain to send the Herodians hurrying to the civil powers to accuse Him of rebellion against Rome. But the plan again ricocheted and fell to the ground. "Pay Caesar what is due to Caesar," countered Jesus, "and pay God what is due to God." The Jew was indebted to both Caesar and God. By having accepted the Roman coinage as a symbol of buying power, the nation had acknowledged Caesar as their sovereign earthly monarch. Therefore, the tribute money was a debt that had nothing to do with their heated religious scruples. They owed it to Rome to provide support, and they owed it to God to submit their lives to His ultimate control. It was apparent that they were trying to get around paying either debt!

While the Pharisees and Herodians moved away like cowed dogs that had just been given a sound thrashing, the next contender came on the scene - the orthodox, conservative Sadducees. Playing their hand from an entirely different approach, the Sadducees began to recount the old law of levirate marriage. This was as good a way as any to change the subject from the payment of taxes to Rome and point out the errors of Jesus' logic at the same time.

Law is not precisely the correct word. Levirate marriage was more a duty of love than an inflexible law. Seldom did any Jew, steeped in the essential solidarity of the family, refuse to comply with this custom. Onan is singled out in the Old Testament as a warning to those who would treat such a custom lightly (Gen. 38:8). In short, this was an arrangement by which a man was assured immortality through his brother and children. The question, simply stated, was which of seven brothers, each of whom had been married to the same woman, would be her husband in the resurrection?

The point of the question was to reveal what they felt to be the irrational nature of the resurrection and thereby put Jesus in a ridiculous light. With not a ruffle of consternation, Jesus plunged into the Sadducees' dilemma with His usual piercing insight. The problem was not in the question itself so much as in the false assumption which lay behind it. The assumption was that, if there should be life in the world to come, it would be simply more of the same. Striking at the heart of their materialistic concept of life after death, Christ blasted both their hopelessness concerning death and their hopefulness in trapping Him by providing a description of the other side that throws much needed light on the subject.

Heaven will be an improvement of earth! When earthly life terminates, the sex drive is annulled. The completed and perfected sons and daughters of God live forever as brothers and sisters (their fundamental and eternal relationship) in one family, whose father and mother is God. This is not to suggest that husbands and wives will not be reunited in full recognition of each other, but it is to say that a more meaningful relationship than any previously existing will prevail in a world where the service of God takes priority over every other interest. This explains the reference to angels, whose prime function is that of service.

As a clincher in the argument between the Sadducees and Pharisees about the possibility of resurrection, Jesus concluded His response to His critics with a reference to Moses at the flaming bush. Having captured Moses' attention with the fire, Jehovah exclaimed, "I am the God of Abraham, the God of Isaac, and the God of Jacob." On the religious authorities' own premise that Jehovah is the God of the living and not the dead, Christ insisted that the Father's own word of identification with the patriarchs left no question about the Hebrew fathers' being alive in another realm.

Discomfited thoroughly by the incisive perception of the "country rabbi," the representatives of the priestly aristocracy withdrew into their scroll-lined towers for further deliberation about this strange teacher who had an answer for everyone. If there were any party so intensely dedicated to the silencing of Jesus as to be unwilling to acknowledge defeat, however, it was the Pharisees. Fresh from the emergency session in the court of the Israelites came a young lawyer reeking with the aroma of suave diplomacy. "Master," he called Jesus, not with the outward contempt which he may have inwardly felt, but with a forced recognition that there was something "masterful" about His ability to get to the heart of every issue. The question which he put to the Lord was tricky but valid: "Which is the first commandment of all?" Out of the original Ten Commandments, the rabbinical schools had created a complex system of moral and ceremonial law. It was all so neatly arranged as to be artistically correct—but humanly impossible to keep.

The conservative Shammaites insisted that every trivial facet of the ceremonial law was as binding as the Decalogue itself. At the other extreme, the liberal Hillelites argued that any command could be unimportant and unavailing, depending on one's attitude. Jesus' answer made it clear that He did not side with either school of thought. Law is fundamentally important, according to the Master, but it must not be allowed to become an intolerable burden.

When Jesus, in one disarming blow, explained the priority of agape love toward God first and one's fellows second, the scribe was left with no choice but to admit that the Lord had wisely summed up the basic divine expectations underlying the complexity of rabbinical interpretations. The man who has this kind of dedication to the Law need have no overwhelming concern about the scrupulous demands of the varied schools of morality. He will fall victim to none of the immorality of an unregenerate society under the disguise of some "new morality," but will rather commit himself to that manner of life which never uses God in the service of man or abuses man in the service of God!

"After this," writes Mark, "nobody felt like asking Him any more questions" (Mark 12:34 Phillips). The scribes, elders, Pharisees, Herodians, and Sadducees had all suffered from their hostile boomerangs as they stood in numinous awe of the wisdom and power of Christ. One can be hit in the head with superior logic only so many times without feeling the dizziness that renders him in no condition to retaliate. But if the churchmen were ready to negotiate a "cease-fire" in that battle of wits, Jesus himself had one more volley to fire.

The most familiar subject in the Jews' theology was the descent of the Messiah. And it was an accepted belief that the Lord's Anointed One would be a direct son of David. Therefore, the Master challenged a belief that was only a half-truth. But it was more than a challenge to rethink a theological position; it was a challenge to recognize the divine identity of Jesus Himself.

I find it impossible to agree with Bornkamm, who says that "behind the doctrinal teaching concerning the Messianic secret there still dimly emerges the fact that Jesus' history was originally a non-Messianic history, which was portrayed in the light of the Messianic faith of the Church only after Easter."[4] Jesus knew His mission from the start.

"Whose Son is He?" inquired Christ of the religious scholars. "Whose Son is this Messiah for whom you are looking?" And when they fell into the error of trying to answer in the customary vein of Jewish theology, they became entangled in a net of logic from which it was impossible to extricate themselves. "If the Messiah is David's Son," which was the reply made by the unwitting churchmen, "then why would David refer to Him as 'Lord'?" continued Jesus. His reference was to Psalm 110, and the argument was launched on the dual premise that the authorship of the psalm under consideration was unquestioned and that its content was messianic.

Only one answer was possible. David would not call his son "Lord" unless the Son was divine. The Messiah was David's son by human descent, but He was God's Son by divine intervention in the process of human genesis. "He was a gift of God to the Davidic house, not less truly, but on the contrary in a more wonderful way, than if he had been descended from David by ordinary generation."[5] Thus, the Messiah could only rightfully be addressed, even by the king, as "Lord." But, as was the usual case, there seemed to be no ready suggestion offered as an alternative solution to the enigma that the Master had proposed. The inability of the leaders to lead was once again made clear to the multitudes.

Although the controversy between Jesus and the leaders of Israel had rendered further attack useless, the Lord was unwilling to let the chance pass for one final round of parables. If He were unmatched in His ability to counter in verbal battle, the Master teacher was also inimitable in His uncanny knack for creating stories on the spur of the moment. According to Matthew's reporting, the three parabolic lessons imparted on this third day in Holy Week came one upon the conclusion of another. To design one such story on impulse would be difficult enough, but to draw out of His heart three similar yet uniquely different parables at once would reveal wisdom beyond the scope of most mortals.

The pretending Pharisees were likened to a son who promised to work in his father's vineyard but never got around to it. The tax collectors and prostitutes were compared to the son who flatly refused and then repented of his impudence and got busy. The tax gatherers and prostitutes had openly rebelled against God until, under the preaching of John, they accepted baptism and changed their living. The Pharisees, on the other hand, had spoken politely so as not to offend in any overt manner and thus, in utter self-righteousness, had refused to acknowledge any failure at all. They remind one of Lewis' cat who, "when he sits and stares you out of countenance he is thanking God that he is not as these dogs, or these humans, or even as other cats."[6]

In the second parable, Jesus told a shocking story about some rude tenants who refused to pay their rent. When the owner of the vineyard sent his servants to collect his due at vintage time, the ungrateful tenants assaulted, beat, and killed them. There was nothing left to do except send his son, whose authority the tenants could not avoid respecting. Their response, however, was the same—and the heir was murdered and tossed from the vineyard.

Lest they miss the point of the parable, Jesus inquired as to whether they recalled the saying in Psalm 118, "The stone which the builders rejected, the same has become the head of the corner." Having abused the prophets and shamefully mistreated the Son, the Jewish church was in no condition to remain stewards of the vineyard or builders of the kingdom of God. At this, the Pharisees bristled again with hostility. "The good repent on knowing their sin; the evil become angry when discovered."[7]

In the third and last parable, the Lord changed from the analogy of a vineyard to that of a marriage feast given by a king for his son. The guests, who had been disposed to accept the earlier invitation (such was the custom in the ancient East), refused at the zero hour to honor their commitment. To insult the king is a serious matter in any language! While the fabulous feast lay untouched on the table, the favored guests continued with their business concerns and personal affairs. "In themselves none of these things and activities are bad," says Thielicke. "As a rule, the road to hell is paved not with crimes and great scandals but with things that are quite harmless, with pure proprieties, and simply because these harmless proprieties acquire a false importance in our life, because they suddenly get in our light."[8]

The application was clear. The "untouchables," who were later invited to fill the seats left empty by people who had been too blessed and coddled to be grateful, were also identifiable. They were the irreligious, the tax gatherers, the harlots, and the sinners with unclean hands and unwashed faces! But, while the sinner is welcome at the marriage feast, he is invited only on the same conditions that apply to the righteous—he must prepare himself for the royal occasion. In this parable, the preparation is represented by the wedding garment. The guest who tried to sneak in without preparation was as bad as the guests who refused to come because they failed to see their need.

"Many are called, but few are chosen," said Jesus, as He explained the strange roughness of the king who had the tin-clothed guest thrown into the streets. God calls everyone to Himself, but even those who answer are put to the test. "Insincerity is robbed of all disguise when the king enters. It has no haven save the poor haven of 'outer darkness.' It is cast forth from the brightness and warmth of the banquet-hall when Jesus plights His troth with those who would sincerely love Him. It is flung into the narrow street which has no light!"[9]

In Luke's chronology of the last week, Jesus is portrayed, probably near the end of the third day's grueling controversies, as observing a refreshing act of sincere worship within the temple (21:1–4; cf. Mark 12:41–44). Sitting at the edge of the court of women, troubled and weary, the Master watched the milling throngs. In the crowd of rich contributors, who were displaying their acts of piety by dropping large offerings into the thirteen trumpet-shaped chests, an impoverished woman approached the aperture of one of the trumpets and timidly dropped in her offering. She had given only two *prutahs*, the smallest gift allowed even for the poorest of the poor.

If there were much to condemn in Jerusalem that day, there was also something to praise. "This poor widow bath cast in more than they all," observed the Lord, "for all these have of their abundance cast in unto the offerings of God: but she of her penury hath cast in all the living that she had" (Luke 21:3–4 KJV). Her act of worship (and true worship always includes a response to God's revelation through giving of ourselves) was so unassuming, so sincere, so acceptable. Ambrose was right when he suggested that God is not interested in what we give but in what we have left.

It was during Jesus' remarks about the widow's giving that the disciples were looking wistfully at the dying beauty of the temple, the huge stones and gleaming gold ornamentation. As they looked about them at an edifice that had been under construction for nearly fifty years and was still incomplete, the Twelve were impressed, as always. "But, it is all coming down," said Jesus. "This Temple shall soon become a pile of ruins!" Naturally, the disciples were anxious to know more about His prediction—the date and attending circumstances. In answer to those disturbing questions, the Master spent the remaining hour of the late afternoon talking about two important matters—the desecration of the temple and the end of the world.

Most likely, the Twelve were confused about all the talk surrounding eschatological themes. When? What? How? and Who? were questions that crowded into the forefront of their minds. Matthew (24:3) recalls that the questions were specifically asked of two events, while Mark (13:4) and Luke (21:7) tend to blend the questions into a single concern—that of the destruction of the temple. The answer that Jesus gave, long and involved as it was, would suggest that the overriding thought in the mind of Christ was that of the end of the world.

Although the predictions about persecution and martyrdom may be considered applicable to Jews in every generation, the sayings about false Christs, international wars, famines, the abomination of desolation, stellar disruptions, and the cloud of glory were intended to prepare the hearts of all disciples in coming generations for the second advent. It is almost certain that the verse "This generation shall not pass, till all these things be fulfilled" (Matt. 24:34; cf. Mark 13:30; Luke 21:32) was a reference to the generation of Jews living when these ultimate signs begin to multiply. Whatever the exact words were, "beware," "watch," "endure," and "pray" are the terms employed by the Evangelists to stress the significant burden of the Lord's message. Thus ended the third day in Holy Week with a Christ who was exhausted by the tensions between God and Satan, a struggle in which He had been all but torn apart.

WEDNESDAY

Then one of the twelve, who was called Judas Iscariot, went to the chief priests and said, "What will you give me if I deliver him to you?" And they paid him thirty pieces of silver. And from that moment he sought an opportunity to betray him. (Matt. 26:14–16 RSV)[1]

And God Rested

In view of the busy days that characterized the earthly life of the Son of God, it is almost impossible to believe that there was ever a time when Jesus was idle. Even his nights were frequently spent in ardent activity in a task which was the most strenuous of all—prayer. Sincere prayer is hard work because it engages the whole person—body, soul, and spirit—in dialogue with the eternal. Wednesday of Holy Week, however, was a quiet day.

Luke records nothing as having happened of any consequence, while Matthew and Mark mention the activity of the scribes and Pharisees, the anointing of Jesus at Bethany, and Jesus' betrayal by Judas. The Lord was not at all involved in the first mentioned action and only passively so in the second and third. It is thought-provoking to realize that even God can become exhausted in dealing with man's rebellion and undisciplined spirit.

The theory which argues that Jesus baited the rulers and Judas into a plan which eventually enabled Him to escape death[2] seems completely incongruous with the facts on this day of betrayal and legal maneuvering. It is not Jesus but the rulers themselves who are trying to bait the trap for the Lord. During the very day when Christ was resting in Bethany, His enemies were in heated planning sessions, attempting to work out a plot that could not fail. The one thing of which they were sure was that the trap must not be sprung on the feast day, when tension would be at key pitch. Everyone with any grievance against the Master was now concentrating his attention and energy on a surefire solution to the *pseudo-Messianic problem*. Pharisees, Sadducees, Herodians, priests, elders, scribes, Annas, Caiaphas, and others not mentioned in the record were all bent on getting rid of the troublemaker once and for all.

Christ knew exactly what was happening. He had known since early in His ministry, possibly even before, that destiny had chosen Him for suffering and death. When Nicodemus came for his nocturnal rooftop conference, Jesus had mentioned something about His approaching death. It was to prepare the hearts of the Twelve that He had spoken of the "entombment" of Jonah as a simile, the removal of the bridegroom and its attendant sorrow, the good shepherd who dies for the sheep, and the murder of the owner's son by wicked tenants who refused to pay their rent. We marvel at the continuous supply of power that He received and also spent day after day. It had been always replenished until now. But now, the long day was over and the darkness had settled upon that little land. The night "when no man can work" of which He had often warned had come. The teaching ministry was ended, and the Son of God was at last allowed to rest.

It was a lull before the storm. There had been many storms to face during those three years. It had all started with the fury of strange and demonic forces that sought to tear apart the freshly ordained Messiah in a tempest of temptation. The storm had struck again that day in Nazareth when His own family accused Him of madness and the townsfolk threatened to throw Him off a mountaintop. When Peter sought to alter His mission into some unordained political messiahship, the winds of evil were high. Several times, well-meaning Jews had sought to put a crown on Jesus' head, and the old wilderness lure to rule an unrighteous kingdom came forcefully back. The conflicts with churchmen, almost daily, were trying, even for one so hardened to storms as He. The easiest storms of all for Him to face were those that so frightened the disciples on the Sea of Galilee. The hardest storm of all was about to break in the upper room, in the garden, and on the cross.

Of all the Lord's dependable friends, none seemed so close and intimate as the family of Lazarus and his sisters. This fourth day of His last week was most probably spent in their home in Bethany. "How they spent it no one knows, but we do know that he had the whole situation clearly in mind and strongly in hand. There were no doubt uplifting talks, purifying prayers, and ennobling fellowship."[3] Only recently had Jesus brought Lazarus back from a four-day journey in the realm of death, and there must have been exciting subjects of conversation that took place between these friends during the long nights that seemed too short to get everything said that pressed for a hearing. To have been allowed to eavesdrop on those private discussions would have been most enlightening on the matter of death, a subject much on the minds of all within that household.

Sometime during that Wednesday, an invitation came to Jesus to dine at the home of one called Simon the leper. Nowhere else is anyone mentioned by this name on the pages of the New Testament. Some have conjectured, since John's account (6:7) names Martha as having prepared the meal and also includes Lazarus and Mary in the repast, that Simon was either the father of these three friends or the husband of Martha. Since John, writing at a much later date than either Mark or Matthew, makes no mention of Simon at all, it is possible that he had died in the interval and that Martha had assumed full responsibility for the household. There is no evidence at all, however, for this fascinating theory.

The more probable speculation is that this host was a neighbor of the Bethany family and had been cleansed of his leprosy by Jesus at some earlier meeting. It is known that the Master cleansed a number of lepers, any one of which may have been Simon of Bethany. Krummacher, the distinguished German pastor of the nineteenth century, states this view clearly.

> All Bethany knows that he had prepared this feast for the Lord Jesus, solely from feelings of gratitude for the marvelous cure which he had experienced through Him; and even His enemies cannot deny that, in this man, a monument is erected to the Lord Jesus, which speaks louder and more effectively than any inscription is able to do.[4]

It was while Jesus, Lazarus, Simon, and probably the disciples were eating that Mary slipped quietly into position behind the Lord, broke open a container of expensive perfume, and lavishly poured its contents onto Christ's head. Such an act was typical of this younger sister, who was possessed with a sensitive spirit. Martha, who was much more practical about life, had been perturbed with Mary once before for sitting at the feet of the Master while she was forced to do the chores. She had even complained to Christ about it, only to be reminded that housework could wait when one was learning about God. So, once again, while the older sister served the dinner, young Mary was emptying a vial of spikenard, for which she had saved a lifetime, on the flowing hair of the Lord.

Some of the disciples were indignant at the wasteful extravagance. John identifies the complaining spokesman as Judas, an identity quite in keeping with his obsession with money, but Matthew and Mark are probably correct in suggesting that the grievance was shared by all the disciples. Almost any of us would have been shocked by such apparent wastefulness. We would have immediately perceived many far better opportunities for using the price of a vial of perfume. "What about the poor?" asked the offended bystanders. "This precious elixir would have brought enough money in the market to feed and clothe a number of people." The three hundred denarii represented the amount of money received by a laborer for nearly a year's work, since one denarius was the wage normally paid for one day's labor. Philip had reminded Jesus on another occasion (John 6:7) that two hundred denarii would be inadequate to feed so large a crowd as that gathered before them. On this basis, we may assume that this perfume would have brought enough in sale to provide a good meal for four or five thousand people.

When Jesus replied to the critical disciples, "Let her alone; why must you make her feel uncomfortable? She has done a beautiful thing for me ... for she has anointed my body in preparation for burial" (Mark 14:6,8 Phillips), He clarified once and for all the fact that money and possessions are never wasted if they are given sacrificially and lovingly in His name. The man who gives $100,000 to install new windows of symbolism in his church is to be praised no less by God than the man who gives as much to a work of mission in the ghettos of New York or the jungles in some faraway land. Neither man will receive the blessing of God if he makes his gift to bring attention to himself. If his motive is to "anoint His body," then one must be cautious about judgmental attitudes of wastefulness.

"You have the poor with you always and you can do good to them whenever you like, but you will not always have me," observed Jesus. "She has done all she could" (Mark 14:7–8 Phillips). There is no question whatsoever that the Lord knew He had only a few hours to live. The world was an open tomb, and the aroma of spikenard was blended with the odor of blood. There was nothing that anyone could do now. The die was cast, and the Lord of glory was already feeling the sting of the thorns and the pain of the nails. But while others talked (and some of them talked pretty big about what they would do to defend Jesus against His enemies), Mary was not content to talk. For her, love was something one did. She would never be able to repay her Master for having given back her beloved brother when all human hope was gone. The perfume seemed such a small thing for so great a blessing. She did what she could, and Christ smiled upon her devotion.

The poor have always been with us. We are constantly aware of their presence and convicted by their sad state. But in spite of any and all efforts toward eliminating poverty—and every honest attempt is Christlike—the poor will be around as long as the world lasts. Many causes are to be found for poverty, not the least of which is unwillingness to work in many instances and unwillingness to share in many others. If all people of means practiced the loving ministry of Jesus to the poor, then the problem could be eradicated overnight. But as Sweazy so well puts it, "There will never be a fair division of profits and wages among materialists ... Society is not saved by the Christian principles of honesty, justice, brotherhood, and love, because there are not enough people—in the United States or in the world—who believe in them."[5]

Certainly this was not Jesus' way of getting out of caring for the poor. Anyone who has given His life more than a cursory study knows better than that. Rather, it was His way of facing squarely the perennial problem of poverty and the certain survival of selfishness. All too well did Christ know that neither Judas nor the other eleven were primarily interested in the poor. They salved their consciences by talking about it and declaring what they would do if they had the means. "You have had many opportunities for helping the poor," implied Jesus, "and you will always have these ready-made openings for service. Do not talk piously about what you would do with Mary's possessions. I have not seen any of you using conscientiously what you yourself have to alleviate the hard lot of the poor!"

Many of us today are critical of the church for spending money wastefully on buildings, organs, carpeting, and carillons when it should be given to the poor. Such criticism bears little weight when we who make the accusations live in luxurious homes, drive fancy cars, and cherish comfortable savings accounts. Like Judas and the Eleven, we, under the pretense of charity, protest against the wastefulness of others in an effort to disguise our own selfish baseness.

Furthermore, we completely misunderstand the poor if they are thought of as being only physically in need of something to gnaw with their teeth or wear on their backs. Are the poor no more than animals for whom we are to provide shelter, raiment, and bread? Important and necessary as these things are, we possess a base notion of them if we imagine that the poor can only eat and drink. Had these three hundred denarii been given to the poor in Jerusalem, the whole world, both rich and poor, would have been greatly impoverished.

Mary's act was one of lavish devotion which refused to count the cost. She was not trying to worship in respectability. To have let drop just a small fragment of the precious nard would have been the respectable thing to do. Everybody would have praised her for it—that is, everybody but God. No one questions the righteousness of the person who gives to the church, but everyone questions the judgment of the person who dares to overdo it! In our comfortable, complacent religion, there is no place left for sacrifice. How refreshing it must have been, and must still be, to Jesus for someone to refuse to count the cost of loving discipleship!

One of the highest accolades ever paid to anyone was paid by Jesus to this misunderstood woman. "Wherever the gospel is preached in the whole world, what she has done will be told in memory of her" (Mark 14:9 RSV). And, sure enough, the Church is still recounting this lovely incident, this "oasis of sweetness in the desert of bitterness,"[6] this light in the black cave of death. We would do well to emulate Mary, for, while there are times when one who always has obligations to minister to the poor is forced to care for temporal affairs, there is never a moment when life cannot be glorified if we live it in utter abandonment at the feet of Christ.

Possibly stung by the rebuke, which he believed to be flung especially at him, Judas watched for a chance to slip away from the dinner party without being noticed. At the very hour when Mary was emptying her savings account onto the head and feet of Jesus, Judas Iscariot was making room in his beggar's basket for the blood money that he had decided to seek. Under the cover of darkness, for night had already come to the little hamlet of Bethany, the man with the money pouch crouched in the shadows of the buildings until he reached the edge of town, where he broke into a nervous run toward the Holy City.

Arriving at the gates of the temple, Judas stammeringly asked the guards to inform the priests that a disciple of Jesus had some information which they would welcome. The guards disappeared into the semidarkness of the temple enclosure, and the frightened disciple waited for what seemed to be an eternity. Every sound was so magnified that the wind in the trees and the footsteps of an approaching dog startled and alarmed him. Never had his heart pounded so heavily within his chest, and never before had he wanted so desperately to run without knowing where to go.

His clammy hands were clutching tightly the bars of the gate when he heard the sound of the guards returning to their sentry posts. They brought news that the priests would see him. Without a word, Judas followed the guide, who had been sent to lead him into the court of the priests. In the flickering light of the lamps, Judas could not tell whether the holy faces behind their beards were hostile or friendly. Later, he sensed that the priests were more suspicious than hostile and that they probably despised him for what he was doing, even though they welcomed his help.

Undoubtedly, someone must have asked him why he had come on this errand of betrayal. It was necessary to cross-examine such a one, lest the priests be led into a well-planned trap. People who are filled with hate are always suspicious of others, even those who are allied with them. What the errant disciple may have told them, we dare only guess. Judas is one of history's most complex personalities, and, after two thousand years, no one has been able to arrive at a final answer as to why this enigmatic friend of Jesus turned against Him at the last moment. Is it possible that he was as black a villain as some have painted him? Could he have been so emotionally disturbed as to be unaccountable for what he was doing? May his intent have been to help Jesus bring the kingdom of God to full fruition? These are questions that have haunted people's minds for centuries.

Luke states that "Satan entered into him" (22:3), apparently believing that it happened that night in Bethany, while John reserves the demonic entry for the occasion of the supper on the following night (13:27). Whatever one may think about the origin and propagation of evil, it seems obvious that both Jesus and His narrators believed in the existence and power of a personal Devil. As Christ had become the incarnation of God in Bethlehem, Judas had become the incarnation of Satan at Bethany!

Striking at his weakest point, Satan appealed to Judas' avaricious nature. Jesus had made it clear that He was going to die, and this grim disciple who had given up everything to have a share in the Messiah's kingdom was not going to be outdone. If the Master were determined to die, then Judas would take advantage of the occasion to add to the money bag. At least there would be something to show for his wasted years with a "false messiah." John was quite certain that this was the sole reason for the dastardly deed of the "disciple despised."

The haggling and disputing went on between the chief priests and the Savior's defector, and the air was filled with loud and angry words—that is, if Judas' prime purpose was money. What they may have offered and what he may have demanded are unknown. It was at last agreed, however, that the ex-disciple would deliver his Master to the enemy for thirty pieces of silver. That was the price of a common slave. Thus, it would seem that, if silver were the motive behind the betrayal, the betrayer would have held out for a higher price. Surely, there could have been no doubt in his mind that the priests would have paid almost any price to be assured of their victim's arrest. Perhaps there were other motives lurking in that strange and twisted mind.

One must recognize that a human mind is a complex and not easily explainable machine. Numerous impressions, childhood memories, hostilities, imaginations, and fears combine to make one act as he does. Is it not possible that Judas may have felt like an outsider all along? He was the only disciple from Judea, and everyone seemed to take note of the fact by tacking onto his name the word *Iscariot*, which designated him as "a man from Kerioth."

The suggestion has been made also that the word *Iscariot* had something to do with the Greek term *sicarius*, meaning "dagger-bearer." The impassioned zealots for Jewish nationalism carried daggers in their robes, which they did not hesitate to thrust into the heart of a Roman or a sympathizer with the Roman cause. Judas has been thought to have been a Zealot before becoming a disciple. It has been further speculated that Judas was jealous of John, the beloved disciple, and wanted the position that he occupied in the heart of Jesus. Perhaps, too, he was sensitive about being reprimanded by Jesus in the home at

Bethany. At that point, he may have been so thoroughly mixed up that he had little control over his aching head.

Most likely, Judas was looking for a political kingdom without national repentance and, believing the Master to be the Messiah, joined ranks with Him, only to be confused at the end of three years. During that time, Jesus had numerous opportunities to accept the kingdom (as Judas understood it) but had refused to act. At last, with the conflict in Jerusalem at key pitch, Judas felt that it was then or never for his Master. Therefore, knowing that Jesus had the power to conquer any foe, the well-meaning disciple believed that all he needed to do was get the Lord into a situation where He would have to use His messianic powers.

He fully expected Jesus to use divine power to blast His enemies and establish the political reign of David with no censure of the Jewish nation's sins. Judas did not think that any harm could possibly come to the Lord. If this suggestion has any credibility, then it means that Judas may have been less a demon than we have thought. Edersheim, in his monumental study on the life of Christ, almost hauntingly brings his remarks about Judas to a close with the question, "And—can there be a store in the Eternal Compassion for the Betrayer of Christ?"[7] It is not for us to say.

While all this was going on in the temple at Jerusalem, Jesus was spending His last night of rest upon this earth until after the crucifixion. Whether He slept or prayed through the night in Bethany, we do not know, but we have our idea. It had been a strange day—the hostile leaders of Jewry laying their strategy for the death of Jesus, Mary lavishly pouring her precious perfume upon His head, and Judas bargaining with the priests to betray Him. Through it all, the Lord rested and awaited the glory that history would give Him. Let the world treat God with love or handle Him with hate, but the end would justify the life. As the rulers clenched their fists in sheer hatred, Mary opened her heart in pure devotion, Judas surrendered his mind to clouded confusion, and the Son of God was offering himself to the Father and the world in the unshaken conviction that the kingdom of God could not be stopped!

THURSDAY

The Son of Man has been honored, and God has been honored, through him, and God will through himself honor him; he will honor him immediately. My children, I am to be with you only a little longer. (John 13:31–33, Goodspeed)[1]

The Day of Suffering Fellowship

If one sticks rigidly to the Jewish calendar, then one must admit that nothing happened on Thursday except the preparation for the Passover Feast and possibly the dastardly bargaining session between Judas and the chief priests. According to Hebrew chronology, a day began and ended at sundown rather than at midnight. By this method of timekeeping, the Passover, as well as the ordeal in the garden, the betrayal, the ecclesiastical and civil trials, and the crucifixion, all took place on Friday. For us, it is much less confusing to end the day at midnight since this is our ingrained habit of counting time. Therefore, we shall place the Last Supper, the garden experience, and the ecclesiastical trial before midnight Thursday. The haggling dialogue between

Judas and the priests will be allowed to remain with the events of the preceding day, since the incident probably transpired before the midnight hour. This being the case, the events of Maundy Thursday will comprise the greater part of three chapters. The "glory" of that day is too extensive to confine to our usually allotted space.

Sometime during this fifth day of Holy Week, the Lord dispatched Peter and John on a mission to locate a suitable place for a rabbi and his disciples to celebrate the Passover. When the draftees inquired as to where their Master would prefer to eat the *Pascha*, it became obvious that He had already made contact with a friend who would provide both a room and a cue for the disciples that would permit them to arrange for the supper in complete secrecy. The signal for which they were to look was a man "bearing a pitcher of water." Such a man would be easy to find, since women were the ones who carried water jugs on their heads, not men! Peter and John must have smiled at the clever and unique manner in which Jesus made His plans.

When the two disciples entered the house, they were advised what to say. To the host they were to say, "The Master wishes to know where the room is to be found in which He will eat the Passover meal with His men." The word that Jesus used was *kataluma*, which described a simple room such as one would find in any common inn for overnight lodging. It was not the nature of the Son of God to demand the best; no *gold room* banquet hall—just a small chamber for a simple meal. And yet that supper was to glorify all future moments of "breaking bread" and render them sacramental! In fact, Barclay may be exactly right when he says, "It remains a definite possibility that Jesus did not intend to institute a symbolic meal, but that he meant that every time bread was broken and eaten, and every time wine was poured out and drunk—that is, at every meal in every house—he was to be remembered."[2]

The more important point to be made is that Christ did not ask for the *anagaion*, the upper room or most honored place in any house. Presumably, the host had previously insisted on the Master's using the upper chamber, and, for this reason, Jesus suggests to His disciples that such will be shown them. But the Master had not asked for or expected such gracious treatment. Since the host had demanded that he be permitted to have everything arranged—the table and reclining couches, the cups and bowls for the wine and *charoseth*—Peter and John had very little to do. They had but to procure the unleavened cakes, the wine, and the mixture for the charoseth paste.

Much debate has revolved around the identity of the host. There are good grounds, however, for the suggestion that this house belonged to the parents of John Mark and was the very place that was to be frequented so often after the crucifixion by the Eleven. In the Acts of the Apostles (12:12), we learn that the house of Mary (Mark's mother) was a regular meeting place for the followers of the Lord. It was His only home in the City of David; hence, Christ had probably called His men together for teaching in her home on numerous occasions. James Stewart reminds us that it was in this room that the disciples were perplexed about the future, later mourned over the loss of Christ, and finally found Him again.[3] Many sacred memories were clustered about in that room.

Even today, after two thousand years of study, there is no complete agreement that this secret meal shared by the Master and His men was an observance of the Passover. Some insist that it was an outgrowth of the *Kiddush*, which was a weekly repast held by male Jews (often a rabbi and his disciples) as a preparation for the coming Sabbath. It was a fellowship with bread and wine. The Passover included the lamb, which was strikingly absent at the Lord's Supper. Of course, it is quite possible that the narrators' silence about the lamb does not preclude the possibility of its having been on the table. Jesus may have refrained from emphasizing it since the bread and wine were considered to be more common to every meal and would, therefore, serve as a better sacrament for coming generations.

Stauffer makes an interesting comment about this absence of a lamb.

> An apostate was forbidden to eat of the Passover lamb, although he was expressly allowed to eat unleavened bread and bitter herbs ... he would be unable to eat a Passover lamb because he would not be permitted to bring a lamb to the Temple for ritual slaughtering ... Jesus was not just any apostate; he was a condemned preacher of apostasy, and a warrant for his arrest had been issued.[4]

Were it the regular Passover Feast, the dish into which the disciples dipped their cakes was filled with *charoseth*, a mixture of nuts, raisins, apples, almonds, and cinnamon sticks. Its purpose was to remind the worshipping Jew, at this highest festival of the year, of the hard lot of his ancestors in Egypt. The brown paste recalled the bricks which the Jewish slaves were forced to make for Pharaoh, and the cinnamon sticks symbolized the straw which they were compelled to find for themselves. The bitter herbs, which were dipped into the paste, emphasized the difficult existence that they all had endured. The deliverance which Christ was about to provide for all people rendered the emancipation of the Jewish nation a historical fact now to be overshadowed by the redemption which the Passover was meant to symbolize. For this reason, our Lord did not mention the use of the *charoseth* as a part of the sacrament that He was instituting.

Hardly had the meal begun when the atmosphere commenced to close in on the Twelve like some heavy hand of fate. "One of you will betray Me!" announced Jesus. Much earlier, He had seen the incipient stages of satanic fever rising within Judas. "Among you hand-picked twelve I sense the developing of a devil!" This was more than just strong suspicion, as Renan suggests, since Jesus knew who the betrayer would be. The disciples had never seen their Master so broken. What a shock that statement must have been, the first words spoken after reclining at the table! No one except Judas had thought of such a thing. "We must compel ourselves to realize," says Carey, "that the Eleven were to meet in total ignorance of all that had been passing through the mind of Judas."[5]

Some of the disciples sat up rigid on their couches; others fell back as though stabbed in the heart. Tears brimmed on the eyelids of John as Peter leaped to his feet with his hand on his sword. Only Judas looked furtively about the room as one whose secret had been revealed. It was to Iscariot's credit that no one suspected him. Every man suspected himself because he knew how unpredictable is human nature. That is, everyone but Simon Peter. The big fisherman never questioned his own loyalty.

When the Savior acknowledged that the betrayer was one who dipped with Him in the charoseth, He was not exposing Judas. Had He done so, Peter would have done more than sever his ear! They were all sharing in that dish, and Christ was saying that it well might be any one of them. Even when the Master said quietly to Judas, "Whatever you are going to do, do it now!" all assumed that he was being sent on some customary errand by the Lord, probably to purchase something for the feast. It was not until much later that they learned he had gone out not to buy but to sell!

Before the dark disciple went out to fulfill his contract with the hostile churchmen, Jesus solemnly raised the bread aloft and, dramatically breaking it before their sad eyes, said, "This is my body." Then, lifting the cup filled with red wine, He even more quietly said, "This is my blood." It was all so strange, so mysterious, so divine, that the gathered disciples ate and drank in silence. They had no idea what He was doing or what it meant. No Passover meal had ever been like this. We, like the Twelve, take the sacrament in our hands with trembling hearts because, though we have the advantage of the cross and the empty tomb, we do not fully comprehend the depth of meaning that is found at the table of grace.

In the gospel of John (13:4–17) is preserved for us the incident of the washing of the disciples' feet, an episode that took place sometime during that evening before the group departed from the upper room. Rising from the table, the King of all the earth draped a towel about His waist and, filling a basin with water from the purification jar standing nearby, proceeded to bathe the dusty feet of the disciples. To wash the feet of twelve men, changing the water each time, would have taken perhaps an hour's time. It was time for reflection. A thousand strange thoughts must have surged through their minds.

No one understood, but no one dared object in the midst of the holy aura that seemed to surround the Master-Servant. That is, no one except Simon Peter, who never managed to keep quiet regardless of the awesomeness of the moment.

"No! No! Lord, you will never wash my feet! Never!" he affirmed. When Jesus made it clear that no man could share His lot unless cleansed by the Lord, the big fisherman quickly blurted out, "Then wash my hands and head as well as my feet!" There were no halfway measures with this big, blundering disciple.

Having laid aside the towel, the Savior drew an unforgettable lesson from the occasion. If the Lord had washed their feet, which was the task of a menial slave, then how much more should they be willing to wash one another's! But most of us would rather tramp on our brother's toes than wash our neighbor's feet! This is why it would have been well if the early church had included within its growing collection of symbols the towel and the basin. The whole episode must serve as a burr to our memories.

"Only love, a heavenly unquenchable love, gives the patience, the courage, and the wisdom for this great work the Lord has set before us in His holy example," writes Andrew Murray.[6] We will not be far afield to surmise that the incident that called forth this dramatic act was the strife which arose among the disciples in the upper room concerning who would be the greatest (Luke 22:24–30). This was not the first time they had argued about leadership, but it was the last time Jesus would be able to shame their pride. The lesson must be as unforgettable as the sacramental meal itself.

John's terse statement, "And it was night" (13:30), by which he designates the time of day when Judas left the upper room, may suggest more than at first is observed. There is no darkness so bleak and black as that which attacks the heart. The world had caved in upon Judas and the night tides of perdition had begun to roll over his perfidious soul. Alas, Judas, not even the torches of the soldiers will give you light to see!

It is Luke who gives us the little incident preceding the bragging pledge of Peter, in which Jesus informs that disciple that He has been praying for him. And what Jesus had been doing for Simon Peter, He does today for all His followers. He had prayed that Peter's faith would remain unshaken in spite of Satan's evil intents to destroy him. Simon all but shamed the Lord for allowing such a thought to enter His mind. Then it was that the Master deflated the sails of the "man with the keys" (Matt. 16:19) by warning that before the second crowing of the cock, he would three times deny having ever known his Lord.

Peter was aghast! "Lord, if I should be called on to die with You, I will never, never under any circumstances, deny You!" Thoughts of his faithfulness in the past—the confession at Caesarea-Philippi, the day-in and day-out devotion, and the protective surroundings which he had lent to the Lord's ministry—clouded his willingness to face squarely his possible weakness in the future. God is not so much interested in what we have done as in what we are going to do. It is an unrealistic and unacceptable boast for one to predict his future by his earlier performance. Most of us know how easy it is to fall on our faces when we live on our laurels.

No sooner had He finished with His prediction about Peter's denial than Jesus turned to the chore of preparing the hearts and minds of the disciples for what lay ahead. "Do you recall," He reminisced, "how I sent you out to preach and heal without money, or scrip, or even shoes? Yet you lacked nothing! Do you remember?" Simon was probably about to speak again when Jesus continued, "The situation has changed. I am soon going to be taken from you and you will henceforth be on your own. From now on you must take your purse, your scrip, and your sword. If you don't have a sword, sell your garment and buy one."

Jesus was explaining to the disciples that they would have to care for themselves in a hostile world. But what about the sword?

Few scholars say much about this tricky statement. It cannot be simply ignored. Some have used these words to prove Jesus' approval of defending oneself against aggression—that there are limits to every "turn the other cheek" philosophy. They are not entirely wrong. No one knows just where to draw the line on defensive action. Most people find some way to justify whatever they decide to do with a hostile neighbor.

Others insist that the Lord must be interpreted in an entirely metaphorical frame of reference—that He is not talking about daggers and swords at all. If this is so, then the whole statement must be so understood. This would mean that He is not advocating the carrying of a purse or scrip either. And that just may be the case. Jesus was more radical than we can imagine in His demands that men love their brothers rather than hate them, and trust their God rather than doubt Him! Christ may well be simply using symbolic language to describe the central truth that He is not going to be with them for a while and that they are going to have to learn to "fight for themselves" and trust God for the impossible.

When the disciples responded, "Lord, here are two swords!" Jesus replied, "It is enough." There was no time for a lengthy explanation. One can almost sense the disappointment in His words when He says, "It is enough," as if He meant, "That is not what I mean. We will not be using swords, anyway. But how can I ever make you understand? Perhaps later!" Certainly, the reference to "enough" did not mean that two swords would be adequate. It is obvious, if He had been referring to the weapons, that more than two would have been needed. He was, rather, speaking of the whole misunderstood lesson.

More than intriguing is the noticeable inclusion by John of four whole chapters of teaching between the exodus of Judas and the departure of the remaining group for the Mount of Olives. Why John gives such detail is not clear, except for the recognized fact that he is basically concerned with an interpretation rather than a simple record of historical events. Immediately upon the exit of the betrayer, the Lord said, "Now comes the glory of the Son of Man, and the glory of God in Him! If God is glorified through Him then God will glorify the Son of Man—and that without delay" (John 13:31-32). The *glory* of which Jesus spoke is a distinctive Johannine expression synonymous with suffering and death. "Christ believed in suffering as the will of God. He had found it in Scripture that the servant of God should suffer ... He knew that thus He must be perfected; and so His first thought was not how to be delivered from it, but how to *glorify* God in it."[7]

The very cross which heretofore had been equated with a curse would henceforth be transformed into a symbol of glory! In his excellent study in Christian symbols, Cardinal Danielou concludes by stating,

> The sign of the cross is seen to have its origin, not in an allusion to Christ's passion, but as a signification of His divine glory. Even when it comes to be referred to the cross on which He died, that cross is regarded as the expression of the divine power which operates through his death: and the four arms of the cross are looked on as the symbol of cosmic significance of that redeeming act.[8]

History has verified the truth of that messianic understanding of the cross as interpreted by John.

If the Eleven were even dimly aware of what was about to take place, then they must have found it impossible to understand how anything of glory could come from the death of Christ. The Master was insistent, however, in His exaltation of the crucifixion in the divine plan of redemption. Later, He prays, "Father, the hour has come. Glorify your Son now so that He may bring glory to you" (John 17:1 Phillips). The *glory* here is clearly related to the provision of eternal life for the people of God, a provision made possible only through the cross. The *hour* of which He spoke was the moment in history toward which all creation had moved—the decisive and divisive moment when man's redemption would come in response to an act of divine initiative. This hour had not arrived at the marriage in Cana when He stated positively, "My hour has not yet come." The *hour of glory* was reserved in the divine economy for the predetermined event of the cross.

In the beloved fourteenth chapter of the fourth gospel, Jesus promises His disciples that, as they have prepared the guest room for Him, He is now on His way to "prepare a place" for them. The "Father's house," unlike the home of Mary, where they were assembled, had "many rooms," and a place of permanent fellowship would be provided there from which there would be no separation. Once again, Christ and the disciples would be together.

Because of the questions raised by a confused Thomas and a dense Philip, the Lord cleared up any misgivings about His own identity as being equated with God. Growing out of the discourse on the forthcoming separation were words of comfort and fortification, words concerning the future role of the Holy Spirit in filling the place vacated by the departing Christ. As often before, the disciples listened in awe as He unfolded the scroll of the future with both warning and hope, predictions concerning the inevitable persecution which they would face and assurance that an unseen ally would be continually available. The one quality of spirit that needed to be cultivated most, urged Jesus, was the agape of God, a love for one another like unto that love which was sending the Son to the cross.

As the hour grew late, Jesus lifted His face to heaven and offered up His High-Priestly prayer, which comprises the whole of the seventeenth chapter of John. This was an offering of the Eleven as a "living sacrifice." If they had failed to grasp the words of exhortation which had fallen from His lips, then perhaps the solemnity of truth spoken in intercessory prayer would sink into their hearts. It was a prayer for purging and direction, for understanding and acceptance, for security and unity, and for faithfulness and fruition. Indeed, it was an inclusive prayer and especially fitting for the concluding of Christ's teaching mission, a kind of holy benediction upon the little nucleus of the kingdom of God.

THURSDAY

When he began to feel distressed and agitated, he said to them, "My heart is sad, sad even to death; stay here and watch with me." (Matt. 26:37–38 Moffatt)[1]

The Night of Divine Sadness

Peter remembered to tell Mark that, following supper and the exodus of Judas, Jesus and His men sang a hymn. This is the only instance recorded of the Lord's having broken into song. Twice we have heard Him weep, but not until now have we heard Him sing. Across the room and out into the night air resounded the deep and resonant voices of the twelve strong men. Since it was customary to sing the Hallel Psalms (114–118) at the observance of the Passover, it is more than likely that some portion of that section in the Jewish Psalter comprised the content of the hymn they sang.

As the last notes died out on the warm, night air, the Lord turned toward the door with the Eleven quietly following Him down the outside stairway and into the open, vacated street.

No one spoke until the group reached the foot of the Mount of Olives, where Jesus explained that they were going to His favorite place of prayer, the garden of Gethsemane. It was here that He had so often communed with the Father. Just inside the entrance, they paused. Eight of the disciples stretched out upon the ground as the Master took Peter, James, and John deeper into the inner recesses of the garden on a mission of eternal significance. Gethsemane means "the oil press" and was probably so named because the owner had located his press right there. Only wealthier people owned private gardens such as this, and, because of the crowded conditions within the city, they were all located outside the city walls on the Mount of Olives. The proud owner of Gethsemane had doubtless given Jesus permission to use his garden. The identity of this rich friend is unknown, but it is not unreasonable to think that he may have been Nicodemus or maybe even Joseph of Arimathaea.

Aware that the ordeal that He was confronting was too intensely personal to be entered into by others, Jesus pointed to a secluded spot where the three could wait while He penetrated even farther into the lonely shadows. "I am so sad I could die," said the Lord. "Watch and pray," He added, in full knowledge that the grueling day had exhausted His men and that they would find it all too easy to fall asleep. Their prayers were needed to reinforce their depleted spirits, and a vigil was necessary against the approaching enemy. Alone with the trees and the angels, Jesus knelt upon the hard ground and, with a heart so heavy that it was a chore to breathe, poured out His supplication before the Father. "Abba, Father," cried the Master, "all things are possible unto thee; take away this cup from me: nevertheless not what I will, but what thou wilt" (Mark 14:36 KJV).

As far as we know, this was the first and only time that God was ever approached as "Abba." This was the Aramaic word used by a child to describe the tender, informal, mutually recognized relationship that had been arranged by birth between him and his father. While the term may be translated "Father," there is a better rendering. One almost hesitates to suggest it, for fear of sounding either blasphemous or sentimental. There is a constant fear among us that people will think of God on a too familiar basis. Unquestionably, the sovereign majesty of God must be kept in proper perspective by man's creaturehood. The relationship that existed between Jesus and God, however, was unique. In light of this, we are somewhat freer with the acknowledgment that this Aramaic word can best be understood when rendered by the more intimate term "Daddy." One can see from this that the prayer of Jesus in the struggle with destiny is to be perceived in an entirely different light than often has been thought.

If Christ were talking with the heavenly Father as a child makes a request of his daddy, then the prayer becomes far more than an act of submission, certainly more than resignation to fate. It was an uninhibited petition like that made by any son who thinks he knows what is best but who makes full allowance for the experience and wisdom of mature years to overrule his desires. With Jesus, it was not just a matter of deferring to the weight of years, however, but the weight of eternity. He knew that the Father's will is always good and that the divine plan must be judged in light of an eternal design, the full fruition of which no one, not even the Son, could foresee. Therefore, "Not my will, but thine, be done" (KJV), was more than a prayer of submission. It was an act of loving trustfulness toward the One who willed only good for all His sons and daughters.

Involving as it did the certainty of the cross, the trustful surrender of Jesus' human life into the hands of the Father was not without struggle. So heavy was the weight of the sin of the world that the Savior was as one trying to live under the pressure of a great millstone. Blood oozed from His pores and dripped onto the hard soil as He "trod the winepress" of the wrath of God against evil. All the blood of Christ was not shed on the cross. The most painful "bloodletting" of all was experienced as He knelt in anguish of soul and faced His solitary battle in the garden of Gethsemane. Here, the real victory was won and Calvary lost its horror.

Every person must find his or her time of prayer and preparation *before* the storm breaks. When the fury of the raging seas is crashing into the boat, it is too late to pray. The reason that Simon Peter and the other disciples were unequal to the tempest that broke over the world that night in the garden and before the High Priest is to be found in the fact that while they should have been praying, they were sleeping. He who can relax during a storm betrays the truth that he has prepared himself while the winds were low. Throughout the trial, which was soon to commence, Jesus was in complete control of Himself because the entire matter had already been settled with the Father and all was now in the Father's hands. The disciples went to pieces simply because such was not the case with them.

"The cup" was a symbol of suffering and affliction. Socrates had been forced to drink the cup of hemlock, an ancient Athenian form of capital punishment. Earlier, Christ had asked two of His disciples if they were able to drink His cup. It was clearly a reference to His approaching death. Lockyer agrees with this fact but qualifies it to mean that Jesus was afraid that the rigors of the week might kill Him before He came to the victorious death of the cross of redemption. "Thus He prays," says Lockyer, "let this cup—the possibility of a death that would not be the tasting of death for every man—pass from me."² This is an interesting but unlikely view.

In that cup were the bitter dregs of the sins of all the world. There was the sin of Adam, that sin which started a chain reaction of evil and rebellion that continues to gain momentum in this far-removed day. There were the sins of kings and peasants, prophets and publicans, priests and harlots—every sin common to man was in that cup. The very thought was enough to force the blood from the brow of the Son of God. It was bitter as gall as Jesus raised the cup to His lips and emptied its contents into the heart of love! "It is not physical death with its cruel and dark accompaniments that Jesus is shrinking from, but a death such as no man before had ever died, and that is, a death from sin"³ This is why He could not meet His death without anguish and distress, as did Socrates.

Three times He prayed that prayer, for He had to be sure that there was no mistake about the will of the Father. There was too much at stake. When, after the final struggle with destiny, He returned to the slumbering disciples, the Lord said, "Are you still sleeping and taking your rest? It is enough; the hour has come; the Son of Man is betrayed into the hands of sinners. Rise, let us be going; see, my betrayer is at hand" (Mark 14:41–42 RSV). How those words must have stung the soul of Simon! It was obvious that he had failed his Master. At the very hour when Jesus needed him most, he had nothing better to do than sleep!

The hour for which He had been born was swiftly approaching, and Christ was cognizant that the preparation that had been made was "enough." Not again did the Master of prayer open His mouth in petition, except for two brief cries on the cross, one while passing through the "blackout barrier," where He felt sin's penalty in being separated from God, and the other when He made final disposition of this world in a handing over of Himself into the Father's keeping. Plans were completed for history's most senseless and brutal murder and, at the same time, eternity's wisest and most loving gift of heaven's purest Son.

It depends on how one looks at the death of Christ as to whether it was tragedy or victory. In the eternal eyes of God and the more sensitive and perceptive minds of people, it was a time of glory. Due to the fact that success and failure are only a hairsbreadth apart, however, it is not readily seen by many, even today, that Calvary was an unqualified triumph.

No sooner had the disciples gotten to their feet and rubbed the sleep out of their eyes than the sound of foot soldiers entering the garden could be heard. Pilate had dispatched a small number of Roman troops to ensure an orderly arrest. Servants of the high priest and other Jewish officials were responsible for the actual taking into custody of Christ. Matthew and Mark mention a "great multitude," which was probably comprised of some of the less stable citizenry who roamed the streets at that hour of the night. "A strange assembly," writes McRuer, "to be at large on the most sacred night of the most sacred week of the year to all Jewish people!"[4] What thoughts may have run through the mind of Simon Peter as he watched the mob of hostile faces surround the Lord, no one can possibly know. Perhaps there were feelings of deep guilt for having allowed such a situation to develop. If he had only stayed awake and alerted Jesus in time! Floods of anger rushed through his blood at the sight of Judas among the enemy. Why had Peter been so dense? Why did he not sense what was going on earlier and do something about the cowardly underground plotting of that despicable fiend?

Judas Iscariot had given the priests the assurance that there would be no error in identifying the Master in the dimly lighted place of solitude. Having tried and failed so many times in their attempts to get Jesus into their hands, the church leaders were taking no chances in their precautionary measures against any slip that would bring the arresting officers back either empty-handed or with the wrong person. The betrayer had agreed upon a signal that would be foolproof—he would kiss the one for whom they were looking. This would not seem out of place, since it was customary for a disciple to greet his rabbi with the kiss of esteem!

There is an old legend that says that James the Less was so much like Jesus in appearance that the kiss of betrayal was necessary, lest the servants of the high priest arrest James instead. Such a fact would help explain why it was so important that Jesus be pointed out so specifically, since practically everyone in the crowd would have seen before so pronounced a public figure as the Lord and, therefore, recognize him at once.

A matter of particular interest is that the usual word for "kiss" is *philien* and that this is the term used by the narrator when Judas promises to kiss the Master. However, when the report is given as to what actually happened in the garden as the betrayer arrived, the word becomes *kataphilien*, which means "to kiss again and again with deep affection." It might seem that the narrator is making more of the moment of betrayal than he should, but he is probably seeking to paint the deed of Judas as black as midnight. It was dastardly enough to betray Christ, but to do it with a kiss of affection, repeated excessively, reveals the heart of an unfeeling, insensitive knave. It was almost as if Judas felt great delight in the treacherous deed.

Reflecting for a moment, however, on the complex motives

that prevailed in the strange mind of the betrayer, we are at once reminded that the repeated kiss may have been Judas' way of assuring Jesus that he was really on His side. If his intention were to coerce the Lord into using His divine power to overthrow His enemies and establish the kingdom of the Messiah, then the display of zealous affection may well have been a joyous anticipation for both Jesus and Judas himself. In that muddled mind, the moment may have been an occasion of tremendous potential for the Master whom he would never see abused or defeated. There was no reason to believe that anything could go awry when all that power lay dormant within the Christ and needed only someone to light the fuse! "The overwhelming bewilderment and maddening irritant to Judas, was that Jesus, endowed with these transcendent powers, restrained them so unaccountably."[5] If Judas did have a noble purpose, then as the officers laid hands on his Lord and led Him away, Judas must have smiled in the shadows at the thought of the surprise awaiting the vicious priests and unsuspecting Roman authorities. And after it was all over, the disciples would thank him, and Christ would probably give to Judas the "right-hand" seat of authority and power.

Not everyone was smiling as smugly as was Judas. Simon was fighting mad. As the crowd began to manhandle Jesus, the impulsive disciple drew his sword and struck at the arresting officer nearest to him. He came close to splitting the enemy's skull, but the aim of Simon was not as good as it might have been, or maybe the intended victim dodged. At any rate, the sword only sliced off the ear of Malchus, servant of the high priest. Turning to the offending but well-meaning disciple, Jesus said, "Put your sword away lest you be destroyed by it. God needs not the defense of man when there are thousands of angelic warriors waiting in the wings of heaven to do His bidding. But the Scriptures of redemption must be fulfilled, and this is God's way of doing it." (Matthew 26:52-54, author's paraphrase).

Luke adds the interesting sidelight that the Savior, in the midst of His own suffering, paused long enough to put the man's ear back in place and probably offer His apology for the impetuous act of Simon. Redding picturesquely describes Jesus as looking for "that missing ear in the grass at Gethsemane," which may be stretching the point for dramatic effect, but his reflection is well put: "Who cares about someone's ear at a time that makes all the difference in the world? Jesus cared, and on His way to the cross He stooped down to pick up someone's ear and put it back."[6] We have yet to perceive fully the depths of God's loving concern for humanity expressed in Jesus Christ!

Offering no resistance, the Savior asked whom they were seeking and, receiving the reply that a search was being made for Jesus of Nazareth, presented Himself as the object of their malicious intent. So startled were those at the front of the crowd that, at this abrupt surrender in calm dignity, they lurched back from the power of Jesus' composure; several men lost their balance and fell to the ground. Shaming the multitude because they were using force to take Him when there had been many opportunities to arrest Him while He was teaching in the temple, the Master quietly offered the life of God to be treated as a thing of naught by a society that could never allow God to live in its midst without inflicting torture upon Him.

No one except Mark remembers anything about an unnamed youth who had a rather frightening experience with the temple police that night in the garden (14:51–52). Since Peter was responsible for the story as written by the earliest Evangelist, it would be thought that Simon had given this information to John Mark. Many scholars prefer to believe that this is the one place in the entire gospel where the writer speaks on his own authority. It is the opinion of many that Mark is here telling his own story—that he was in the shadows of the olive trees, watching the activity taking place before his eyes. When the officers saw him, they laid restraining hands on him—only to lose their prey as, in abject fear, he fled out of his linen cloth and ran naked out of the garden.

At that time, Mark was too young to be a chosen disciple, but he was intrigued by the suntanned rabbi and His men, who met often in his mother's house. While Mary thought he was asleep, the curious boy was peeping into the upper room where Jesus broke the bread and poured the wine. He had seen Judas depart and later return, where it was believed that Jesus would still be cloistered with His men. The lad overheard the loud talking in the street and gathered from the exchange of words between Judas and the spokesman of the high priest that the crowd, thwarted here, was heading for the garden to try to find and arrest the Master. Grabbing up the linen cloth to cover his body, Mark rushed out into the night to warn Jesus. When Mark got to the garden, the Master was praying, so he dared not interrupt Him. While he waited in the quietness of the trees, the crowd appeared, and then it was too late to warn the Lord. If Mark were not there in the shadows while the others slept, then how are we to explain the fact that we know the words of Jesus' prayer? There was no one else to hear them.

The unruly mob pushed Jesus out to the road and then headed toward the city gate and, eventually, the palace of Annas. It was not far, but there was no time to waste, for the night was well along. What the Jewish high priest would do must be accomplished in short order before the people were awake and prepared to cause trouble. Everything was in order as Annas stood at the window of his quarters, looking down upon the approaching string of torches. At last, at long last, the troublous pretender to the throne of Israel was in his hands, and he would never let Him go until His death was assured.

THURSDAY

Their judgment was unanimous: that he was guilty and should be put to death. Some began to spit on him, blindfolded him, and struck him with their fists, crying out, "Prophesy!" And the High Priest's men set upon him with blows. (Mark 14:64–65)[1]

The Night When the Priests Defied God

Only a passing note is made, and that by John, of Jesus' having been taken first for interrogation to Annas. The official position of high priest belonged to Caiaphas, son-in-law to Annas, but the power behind the throne still resided in the older, crafty, calculating ex-leader in Israel. The Jews still regarded the older priest as the God-appointed potentate. "Annas was deposed from the priesthood by the heathen Roman power; which could not, in the eyes of the Jews, give or take away a sacred and spiritual office. Therefore, it was but natural that the strong Jewish police force, that went to arrest Jesus, should lead Him to Annas first."[2]

What happened in the palace of Annas no one knows. After a cursory examination that satisfied the hostile father-in-law, the victim was forwarded to the younger yes-man under orders of rigid security. John's gospel seems to indicate that the ecclesiastical trial was almost a private affair, with only a few servants and officers present. The Synoptics suggest that the trial was open to the whole Sanhedrin, who questioned Jesus at great length.

There was no real effort to get at the truth in the case before them. Their minds were already made up. Jesus was guilty, and nothing needed to be done now but accumulate the evidence to take to the Roman court. Indeed, there was nothing even faintly just in a trial where the judge, jury, and witnesses had fully decided on the verdict of guilty before the first trace of evidence to corroborate such a suspicion had been given. Jesus was considered guilty until proven innocent, and no one was to be allowed to serve as counsel for His defense! History has long since labeled that ecclesiastical farce as an example of blatant injustice and open illegality.

To begin with, the trial was held at night, which was a breach of Jewish law. It was not in the proper meeting place, the Hall of Hewn Stone, and thus was out of order. The witnesses could not agree on the charges. Words spoken by Jesus were twisted about in an attempt to make them incriminate Him. The high priest was guilty of asking what attorneys call "a leading question." The religious leaders had continuously accused Jesus for three years of breaking their laws and traditions. On the night when they had Him in their power, none of the Jewish hierarchy hesitated to break any or all laws! The laws and regulations were sacrosanct only as long as they served the selfish personal ends of the proud rulers.

When, in desperation at Christ's silent composure, Annas demanded, "Are you the Messiah, the Son of the Blessed One?" the Lord finally broke the silence with His "I am!" As difficult to accept as this may be for those who reject Jesus' messianic consciousness, there was no hesitation for the Lord when asked to identify Himself.

> Here you have the great confession. What an affirmation is this! It lifts us up above all doubt and apprehension. It places our faith on an everlasting foundation. It establishes and seals our entire redemption, and is the grave of every scruple … It was impossible that it could be more clearly testified who Jesus was than was now done.[3]

Although earlier, Jesus had been reluctant to identify Himself, now He was fully frank about who He really was. Indeed, He had come as the King to establish the righteous reign of David, but the nation wanted the reign without the righteousness. This Jesus could not sanction. He would return to the Father's house for a season, after which the kingdom would be established at His second advent.

If any question had played in the minds of the scribes and elders before, then Christ's answer erased it. Recognizing Jesus' self-disclosure as being the equivalent of the one title that Yahweh (Jehovah) reserved for Himself, the Sanhedrin had no doubts concerning the diabolical perversion of this irreverent pretender. For Jesus to respond with "I am" (*Ani Hu*) was to suggest that He was to be equated with the God of Moses, the great I AM. When the stuttering, excuse-finding Moses complained about being sent to Pharaoh and the enslaved Israelites without proof of the proper "organized backing," God said, "Tell them that I AM [*Ani Hu*] has sent you." In using this ancient sacred title, an expression of eternal being, the Master was declaring Himself to be greater than Moses and the prophets and equal with God.

As if He had not already said enough, the Lord hastened to add, "You will see the Son of Man seated on the right hand of God and coming with the clouds of heaven" (Mark 14:16). The literal translation is "right hand of *the Power*," and most translators render the word *dunamis* in this way. Luke expands the phrase to become "right hand of the power of God" (22:69), or, as *The New English Bible* puts it, "Almighty God." What Christ was saying was simply that the position of authority (right hand), second only to the Father, would soon be conferred upon Him. Such a place in the kingdom was recognized as a right to power, a share in the divine rule. And the "clouds of heaven," which were to serve as a conveyance for His advent, had definite eschatological connotations and referred to the second coming of Christ in the power of God to establish the absolute reign of Yahweh and to destroy the works of unrighteousness.

Heim likens the imagery used by Jesus to the dream of Nebuchadnezzar in which a stone came rolling down the slopes to destroy a world colossus.

> We can summarize the event which Jesus predicted as follows: all the world powers which have so far battled in history will be robbed of power, and the One to whom God has given world dominion will come "with the clouds of heaven." Christ will come forth from the cloud of invisibility which has so far concealed Him

and will assume world dominion. The little stone that struck the colossus of the world powers so that they were destroyed will become a great mountain and fill the whole earth.⁴

There was no misunderstanding of the meaning of *cloud* in this connection, since it had always been recognized as the divine vehicle. What Christ had said was considered blasphemy, and the charge carried with it the death penalty.

No further witnesses were needed. Jesus had flung down the gauntlet and it had sealed His death. C. F. Chase, rector of St. Andrews by the Wardrobe, wrote long ago, of the result of the Jewish Council's trial of Jesus,

> They fail to condemn Him on the charge of being a malefactor; but they succeed in condemning Him on the charge of blasphemy. And the blasphemy consists in this, that in the high and appropriate sense and meaning of the title, He declares Himself to be—"THE SON OF GOD."⁵

The strategy of the Jews had, at last, been successful.

While Jesus had been able to evade their deceptive snares and escape their well-designed traps on every prior occasion, at last He had fallen into the biggest snare of all—He had called Himself God! The Sanhedrin was well aware that, since the coming of Rome to power, it had no legal right to put any person to death. The purpose of the ecclesiastical trial was to accumulate enough evidence against Jesus so that a civil trial would become necessary. It would be an easy matter, after such a confession from Jesus, to so work up the Jews as to twist the evidence into charges of sedition. The die was cast, and the president of the Great Sanhedrin, while tearing his robes in presumed holy horror, laughed inwardly with satanic glee!

A bright fire was burning in the lower level of the palace, and around it had congregated a number of the lesser officers and servants. Standing in the group was a stranger to the cohorts of the high priest. He was obviously a Galilean, for the accent of his speech gave away his origin. Nobody seemed to know who he was, but it was easy to see that he was extremely nervous and jumpy. History has identified the stranger for us as Simon Peter. He had followed Jesus all the way to the palace of Caiaphas, but he had kept his distance because of his reputation. Whether the night was cold and the fire was needed for warmth or whether it was only dark and the glowing flames were necessary for light, we cannot say. Simon, however, needed the heat of the fire to warm himself and dry the perspiration from his nervous, clammy hands. It would take more than a bonfire to warm his cooling discipleship.

Suddenly, one of the chambermaids from the palace recognized Peter as having been with Jesus of Nazareth, and her accusation so frightened him that he forgot his former pledge of loyalty and replied, "I have no idea what you may be talking about!" Shocked and disappointed with himself, Simon turned and walked onto the porch, where the light of the fire would not so readily identify him. Perhaps, away from the crowd and in the gray shadows, he could get hold of himself and collect his thoughts. But hardly had he made his exit before the young girl again saw him and more emphatically insisted that the stranger was indeed one of the followers of the Man on trial. The fact that the cock had crowed just as he walked onto the porch had apparently not registered, and Simon quickly reaffirmed his earlier statement. Sometime later, the suspicious bystanders once more mentioned his association with Jesus and called attention to Peter's Galilean speech.

That was the last straw. Matters were getting out of hand, and the disciple saw that he was in great danger. He would swear; that ought to do it. Whether he merely used profanity or rather used the name of God in an oath of truthfulness is uncertain. Possibly he did both. We can almost hear him say, "May the Lord whiten my beard and cut short the years of my life if I be not speaking the truth!" On his face were traces of great anger mixed with fear as, for the second time, he heard the cock crow. As if some magic spell had suddenly been cast about him, his countenance abruptly changed from anger and fear to shame and remorse. And from his eyes, man-sized tears began to fall. Running from the palace, Simon fell upon the ground with his face in his calloused hands. All the fountains of his soul were broken up and the heinousness of his deed swept over him as he realized the stark reality of what he had done.

Normally, the cock crowing is thought of as being the instinctive welcome to the dawn provided by the early-rising barnyard rooster. There is reason to doubt this usually accepted interpretation in the light of Jewish history. It is much more probable that what Peter heard was the sound of the *gallicinium*, which is the Latin word meaning "cock crow" but which describes the blowing of a ram's horn at specified intervals of the night.[6] Since the guard was changed at three o'clock each morning, at which time the gallicinium was sounded, this would tend to pinpoint the hour of Simon's final descent into apostasy. It is Luke who adds the note that, at this moment, Jesus "turned and looked straight at Peter" (22:61). Simon remembered the solemn word of warning that Christ had given him in the upper room.

Meanwhile, John, whom tradition says was well-known to the high priest because he delivered fish to the palace, had been admitted into the inner chamber of Annas, where the trial was in process. This explains why the fourth gospel records several details which the Synoptics fail to include. When John wrote his narrative near the end of the century, he felt it to be wise to add any information that he could personally remember and that would be helpful to the church. He distinctly remembered that dialogue between Jesus and Annas about disciples and doctrine. The high priest had asked for an explanation of Jesus' teaching and a clarification of His intentions as well as some clear word of identification as to whom and where His disciples were.

No response was to come from Jesus except the reminder that nothing had ever been said in secret. To give information about His men was the last thing He would do, for it was not in His plan to have them arrested. The multitudes had heard His words, probably some of those standing in the room with Him, and any one of them could have related exactly what had been taught and preached. This was not an attempt to be curt, though it may have been the Lord's way of condemning Annas for being so adamant in his opposition when he had never once so much as bothered to go to the trouble to hear the words of Christ for himself. Standing by, however, was an official of the court who, desiring to ingratiate himself with the high priest, struck Jesus across the face for what he considered an irreverent remark.

To so abuse a defendant who had no counsel was illegal and inhuman. Therefore, the Master, in complete control of the situation, reminded the abusive officer that he would have his chance to witness against the "hostage in chains" if anything unacceptable had been spoken to the high priest. At any rate, there was no reason for anyone to take the law into his own hands and attempt to judge, sentence, and execute. Jesus was serving as His own counsel for the defense, as none had been provided for Him. Judas had betrayed, Peter had denied, and all the disciples save John had fled into the darkness, as did young John Mark before them. With no legal defense and no physical support, it must have been refreshing for the Master to know that, at least, the moral support of His youngest disciple was not far away.

FRIDAY

And as Pilate wanted to satisfy the crowd, he set Barabbas them, and after having Jesus flogged handed him crucified. (Mark 15:15 Phillips)[1]

The Morning When the State Deserted God

There is no doubt that Judas Iscariot was in close proximity to the palace of the high priest during the trial of Jesus before Annas and Caiaphas. He had watched the milling churchmen and their servants as they wandered in and out of the courtyard. The delay had confused him even more than the failure of Jesus to react with power when arrested in the garden of Gethsemane.

As the first rays of dawn broke across the ancient city, the Master finally emerged from the palace. Judas could not believe his eyes. Jesus was still wearing the chains. Nothing was going as had been planned. The Lord had not declared His kingdom with power. It was perfectly obvious that the guards were on their way to Pilate with the prisoner. What had gone wrong he could not imagine, but Judas literally went to pieces as his plans aborted one after the other. In desperation, the betrayer ran from his hiding place in search of the priests. Without question, he hoped that he would be able to right his wrong at that late hour and convince the authorities that Jesus was not guilty and should thus be released.

The knowledge of his deed and the magnitude of his crime were more than his spirit could bear. Like a frightened animal, Judas burst into the private quarters of the priests and breathlessly blurted out his confession of monstrous guilt: "I have sinned, I have brought an innocent man to his death" (Matt. 27:4). This was Judas' biggest mistake, his fatal blunder. If he had only fallen at the feet of his Master and asked forgiveness, instead of at the feet of the priests! Maclaren stated it beautifully long ago: "The Master did his best by Judas, and would fain have saved him from himself. He kept Judas by His side after the character of the man had appeared. ... If, at this last moment, he had cast himself on his Master's mercy, we should have mentioned his name today—the chief sinner saved."[2]

In a sense, Judas' sin was no greater than was Peter's. The difference was in the way each man responded to his inner guilt. Peter brought his sins to Jesus, while Judas sought consolation from his newly made companions in evil. Man's new lease on life comes from only one source—the forgiving love of God in Christ! There is no question but that Jesus would have forgiven Judas. We have yet to learn how forgiving is the love of God.

Flinging the money down on the gold-covered table, Judas was now possessed with the sudden realization that he had sold himself. Evil men were using him to further their hateful ends against the Master. Perhaps if he returned the money to the priests, the priests would return the Christ to him and he could then make the needed amends. But Judas should have known better. To the religious leaders, there was no amount of money in the world that would be acceptable as bail for the blasphemous prophet who had eluded them so often. The disciple had simply made a bad bargain, and history would never find a way to rectify it.

For churchmen, the priests were rather calloused with their reply: "This is no longer our problem, fellow! It's yours, Judas! Take care of it as best you can." We shudder. But it should not surprise us that religious people who had deliberately set out to destroy one man would not be concerned about saving another. Judas was a cog in the machinery, a tool for a job, a means to an end. He had served his purpose and was now dispensable. It was ever thus. The Church of God must examine itself often to see if men are being used to serve the institution or if the Church is dedicated to aiding men.

Exactly what happened to Judas after his rejection by the priests, we do not know. Matthew alone tells us of Judas' act of returning the money. In his second volume, Luke speaks of Judas' "falling headlong ... and all his bowels gushed out" (Acts 1:16–20). Matthew dramatically portrays the betrayer hanging by the neck, and it is not at all difficult to see how both, the first gospel and the Acts, fit together. One needs only a little imagination to see Judas removing his girdle, tying one end around a gnarled tree limb and the other around his neck, then swinging over the cliff's edge until the knot slips and his body plummets down upon the sharp rocks. There are several early traditions concerning the manner of the traitor's death, but the essence of the suicide is best understood in the light of Matthew and Luke.

At the very moment when Judas was feeling the full impact of his sin's penalty, Pontius Pilate was just beginning his own plunge into the abyss of remorse. Standing before him in the prisoner's docket was a brown-skinned Jew. From the outset of the trial, Pilate felt uneasy. He could not put his finger on the reason, but something about the atmosphere surrounding the whole case was not right. Now that the accused stood calm and erect before him, it was all the governor could do to look the victim in the face. Trying to get ahold of himself, Pilate asked the first question that came to his mind, "Are you the King of the Jews?" It seemed such a silly thing to ask of one so clearly peaceable in appearance. The inquisitor was rather amused, except that the scribes and Pharisees wore expressions of contempt, which left no room for levity.

Religious charges of blasphemy concerned Pilate not in the least. There was only one question that he could ask, and that concerned the rumors about Jesus' claim to be some kind of messianic king. In the unified empire of Rome, there was no place for nationally appointed rulers, especially not in the explosive little nation of Israel. If there were any truth to the accusations of messianism, then it would be Pilate's responsibility to discover it and put an end to any potential uprising before it got off the ground.

Each of the Synoptic writers indicates that the Lord's reply was simply, "You have said this." Possibly, Jesus is dealing here with the confusion of double meanings. Indeed, Christ was the King of the Jews, but His concept of that kingship was quite different than Pilate's. John elaborates this answer into a counter-question: "Is that your own idea, or have others suggested it to you?" (John 18:34). If Pilate were asking about the kingship of Jesus on the basis of hearsay, that question was loaded with false ideas. If he were concerned personally about Christ's identity, that was a different matter.

Pilate explained that, not being a Jew himself, he knew

nothing other than what he had been told by the leaders of Jewry. He was only repeating what he had heard. Then, plainly, the procurator of Judea asked, "What have you done, anyway" (John 18:35 Phillips)? At that point, Jesus gave His only clear-cut defense before the Roman official. Matthew and Mark suggest that the Lord made no response, but John (the only disciple who heard the proceedings of the civil trial) remembers hearing Jesus explain the nature of His kingly role. "My kingdom is not a political regime. If it were, those who are my subjects would fight like true soldiers to prevent the capture of their king," said Jesus. "Then you really are a king!" interrupted Pilate. "Of course, I am a king," replied the Lord. "I came to show men the Truth and the true seeker will recognize it in Me."

Even within the Church today, strange though it may seem, are those who disparage the concept of Christ's kingship. The vogue today is to get Christ off a throne and set Him in the midst of the people as an equal to whom the Church is willing to grant the status of leadership. The sovereign majesty of God in Christ, which was so poignantly described by John of Patmos, is a concept that some no longer find acceptable.

But Jesus unquestionably thought of Himself as a King with total authority. His refusal to be made a king by the masses earlier in His ministry sprang from the same rejection of false political hopes as did His caution about acknowledging kingliness before Pilate. But there were no inner misgivings with Christ as to who He was and what He had been sent to do.

With a sneer that betrayed the politician's skepticism, Pilate, Jesus' antagonist, asked, "What is Truth?" The question was legitimate, although perhaps rhetorical. Multitudes are still undecided as to whether there is any absolute truth. Practically everything has become relative. A whole system of morals has grown up in which both sociologists and theologians are demanding freedom from all rigid laws and regulations. At the same time, others are reacting with the insistence that truth is unchangeable. The rub is in determining what that basic truth is and what are only traditional accretions or interpretations.

When no answer was forthcoming from the lips of Jesus, Pilate went out to the Jews and confessed his own failure in finding reason for condemnation. It may well be that the silence of the Lord on the issue of truth was due to His intuitive ability to detect the obtuseness of the questioner. There is a moral law written within every man, and he who is open to the truth will be aware of it when he is confronted by it. No one ever receives the unadulterated truth as long as he excuses himself from doing it on the pretense that everything is nebulous and unclear.

Wishing to get himself off the hook by subscribing to a Jewish custom, the governor offered to release Jesus at the dawn of the Passover. Just why he thought the crowd might be ready to acquit the Man on trial at this point is anyone's guess. Whatever his hopes, the people in the courtyard dashed them to the ground with their demanding shouts for the release of Barabbas. This man was an insurrectionist guilty of murder. If there was any one prisoner whose freedom would be a threat to the peace of Israel, it would be Barabbas.

Tradition claims Barabbas' given name to have been Jesus. We do know that Barabbas was not actually a name but a patronymic that served much the same purpose as one's family or surname today. It was a combination of *bar*, meaning "son," and *abba*, translated as "father." The full word identified this prisoner as the "son of Abbas" or the "son of the father." The Lord and the murderer having the same name, Pilate may have been the victim of a play on words. As if it were not confusing enough to have to deal with Jesus of Nazareth, who was said to be the Son of God, Pilate had this head-scratching enigma of making a decision between two prisoners with the same name. Both men were named Jesus, and both could have been called Barabbas.

Pilate then ordered that Jesus be scourged. This was a cruel flogging inflicted with a whip made of many thongs, on the end of which were tied sharp, cutting objects. When the beating was over, a prisoner's back was a mass of bloody flesh. Often, men died from the scourging alone. Perhaps the disturbed governor hoped that the sight of Jesus so mutilated and abused would call forth enough pity to get Him freed. But he underestimated the strength of blind prejudice under the impetus of mass hysteria. It would take much more than a heartless beating to change the minds of these evil men.

Pilate, political coward that he was, tried every loophole he could think of to get around taking responsibility for the fatal decision. Hearing that Jesus was a native of Galilee, the governor of Judea immediately sent his prisoner to Herod with greetings and best wishes. But Herod was unable to break the silence of the accused by the accusations of the priests and the questions of the tetrarch, and Jesus was turned over again to Pilate. Before leading Jesus away, however, the soldiers mockingly costumed Him in royal robes and contemptuously made fun of Him. Matthew, Mark, and John place the mocker in the palace of Pilate rather than before Herod, but all four narrators recall the humiliating treatment.

To complicate matters even more for the governor, a message came to the judgment seat from Pilate's wife concerning a disturbing dream that she had experienced. She felt that her husband should refuse to get more deeply involved with the famous prisoner. Therefore, once more, Pilate sought to change the minds of the Jews. "Here is the man!" he shouted, as the purple-draped, thorn-crowned, broken, and bleeding prisoner appeared again before them on the balcony. The answer was, as before: "Crucify Him!"

Exasperated with their angry refusal to be reasonable, the governor turned away in disgust as he shouted, "I do not find anything deserving of death. Take Him and crucify Him yourselves. I will not be a party to your injustice." Pilate well knew that there could be no crucifixion unless he signed the death warrant. This was only another attempt at getting out of his responsibility. "He ought to die," cried the priests, "because He has called Himself the Son of God." The departing governor stopped dead in his tracks as though the full impact of that claim had just dawned on him.

"Where are you from?" he asked of the prisoner, as he slowly turned half round so as not to be forced to look directly into the eyes of the pitiable creature before him. "What does this charge mean? I do not understand. Are you actually laying claim to some divine origin?" Still, no answer escaped the lips of the accused until Pilate reminded his prisoner that it would be to His advantage to say something, since His destiny was in the hands of the governor of Judea. "You would have no authority at all," replied Jesus, "if God had not lent it to you to be dispensed with justice ... Yours is a serious job conferred upon you by the powers of heaven. You are only doing your duty. The greater sin is that being done by those who are accusing Me."

Not until the vicious priests reminded Pilate that he was being disloyal to Caesar by defending a pretender to the throne did Pilate slump, defeated, in his regal chair. The Jews had made it appear that they were more loyal to Rome than was Pilate when they exclaimed, "We have no king but Caesar." If there were any blasphemy that day, it was not spoken by Jesus but by the priests who disowned the kingly rule of God among His chosen people.

There was nothing else to do. The gospel of Matthew alone implies that the restlessness of the crowd was growing into a potential riot. The governor decided it was better to sacrifice Jesus than to let the situation get out of hand. He might incur the wrath of Rome and lose his position for failing to keep the peace.

One of history's saddest scenes is that of Pontius Pilate's washing his hands in a dramatic act of self-absolution before the people. Lady Macbeth, following her foul deed of murder, was more realistic when she woefully cried, "All the perfumes of Arabia will not sweeten this hand."[3] There was no way for the governor to clear himself. Until this very day, the world is not allowed to forget what he did. His name has found its way into the creed, and masses of worshippers speak it in shame every week. And neither did Pilate forget. Legend says that he grew old with a blank stare in his eyes. When Jesus of Nazareth was mentioned, he could not remember His name, yet he spent a quarter of an hour every day just washing his hands!

From Pilate's hall of judgment, Jesus was forced to carry the heavy crossbeam, to which His hands would be nailed, through the city and up the narrow passageway where stood the bazaar, and then to the place of execution just outside the city gate. Fresh blood ran profusely from the deep gashes in His back to mingle with the huge clots that had dried in the arid wind. We wonder that He was able to bear the cross at all after the merciless beating and the rigors of the night. The fact that the Savior could do so was convincing proof of the manliness and strong physical constitution of the One who has so often been erroneously portrayed as a "pale Galilean." None but a muscular and toughened man could have carried his cross so gallantly.

When Jesus had borne His burden as far as He could, the masses who lined the narrow street swimming before His eyes, the Lord fell beneath the weight. One of the onlookers was conscripted to give assistance. The draftee was a dark-skinned man from North Africa who had come to celebrate the Passover. Having no interest in what was happening to Jesus, Simon of Cyrene may have felt insulted at being forced to share a prisoner's cross. Life has a way, however, of playing tricks on us. What Simon resisted that day came later to be the most significant event in his life and a deed never to be forgotten or allowed to go unnoticed by the Christian Church. It is not simply imagination to suggest that Simon was to become a believer before leaving Jerusalem, that he carried the gospel to North Africa, that he led his sons named Rufus and Alexander to Christ, and that Rufus was later to become a leader in the church at Rome (Rom. 16:13).

Weeping women lined the roadway, lamenting loudly as the procession passed. "Do not weep for Me," said Jesus, as He paused in His journey, "but weep for yourselves and your children." The Jews had exonerated dastardly Pilate when he washed his hands, by assuring him that the blood of Jesus would be on them and their children (Matt. 27:25). They had said more than they understood. And now the Master warned the families of these men who stood by the wayside that what they had been so glibly committed to by their husbands and fathers would soon come to pass. Weeping was in order, but not for Jesus. His would be victory; theirs would be defeat—total and irrevocable.

FRIDAY

And they crucified him. (Matt.27:35 KJV)[1]

Mission Accomplished

Crucifixion remains one of man's most cruelly devised methods of execution. Such had not been the customary mode in Jewry, where offenders deserving the death penalty were stoned to death, but it had been adopted without choice when Rome, which had taken the practice from the Phoenicians and Carthaginians, came to power. Traitors, murderers, and incorrigibles were put to death by Roman law by being hanged on crosses erected in public places, where the shame would be worse than the suffering. The cross was an accursed thing to the Jews and a symbol of the worst evil in society. Therefore, no one pitied a man on a cross, since it was acknowledged by all that offenders found thereon were deserving of the treatment.

Death by crucifixion was not always effected in the same way. At times, the malefactor was tied to the crossbar and left suspended in that position until he died from starvation, thirst, and exhaustion. Usually, however, victims were nailed to the cross, their arms stretched out and pinned to the transbar with large spikes while their feet were crossed and thrust through with one great pin. With the weight of the body pulling on the aching hands, the sufferer pushed himself up with his bleeding feet until the pain became so intense that he was forced to swing once more on the nails through his hands. In the slumped position, arms pulled upward, breathing was almost impossible. Thus, it was one continuous up-and-down movement—muscles aching, tendons tearing, and nerves screaming—sometimes for days, before welcome death finally came from loss of blood, physical exhaustion, and suffocation.

The upright, to which the crossbar was fastened, remained on Calvary's hill between executions. It was laid flat on the ground as both victim and the bar were nailed to it. Then, with the combined strength of several Roman soldiers, the cross with its burden was raised into the air and dropped into the hole. With the sudden impact, as the upright struck the hard earth in the bottom of the socket, the flesh tore around the newly made wounds in the sufferer's hands and loud cries of excruciating pain rang out from his lips. But the Master was heard only to say, "Father, forgive them; for they know not what they do" (Luke 23:34 KJV). That prayer was for all who had acted in ignorance: the fleeing disciples, the soldiers, the mob, the priests, Pilate, Herod, Caiaphas, Annas, and all coming generations who would have any part in the sin which nailed Christ to the cross.

It is undoubtedly true that neither the Jews nor the Romans would have crucified the Lord of glory had they known who He was. What they did was done in blind ignorance, and our compassionate Savior knew this to be so. At that agonizing moment in the earthly life of the heavenly King, there was no thought of revenge or hostility. The first thing Jesus did when

He went to His cross was to get immediately to the supreme task of redemption. Already, the Savior had commenced His work of reconciliation between God and man.

William B. Cannon wrote about this moment of quiet forgiveness in death as follows: "Not only did He die in silent protest against human wickedness which slew Him but also in expiation of that wickedness so that the prayer He uttered upon the cross, 'Father, forgive them; for they know not what they do,' He in reality caused to be fulfilled."[2]

Only one act of mercy was allowed at the cross. Some of the women in the city had taken it upon themselves to have a kind of drugged wine available for the dying men.[3] The mixture was never allowed to be strong enough to completely anesthetize the victim, but at least it helped to dull the pain, which was almost unbearable. Jesus' refusal of the tonic can be understood only as we remember that His death was a "tasting of death for every man" (Heb. 2:9). He could not bear our penalty for sin unless He felt the full force of its power. Full and complete consciousness was an unavoidable necessity if the cross were to be redemptive, if the cup were to be drained to its bitterest dregs, and if the horrors of judgment against sin were to be met and overcome.

In the midst of all the suffering, there were soldiers at the foot of the cross who were having a summer picnic gambling for the Lord's seamless robe. The masses, passing before the spectacle of agony, joined the priests in mocking the dying Savior. Jeering at Him in His agony, they challenged the Master to come down, to show His claimed power by descending from the spikes that held His hands to the cross. "He saved others, but He cannot save Himself," snarled the churchmen, and, though the remark was meant to be vicious, it was the highest accolade ever paid to the Son of God.

Indeed, Jesus could have come down from the cross and shattered His enemies like an army of china dolls. But had He done so, the Savior would not have saved others. In the conclusion of his contribution to the *Scottish Journal of Theology*, Markus Barth says, "The New Testament does not grind out empty phrases when it proclaims that the life and peace, righteousness and freedom, joy and fellowship of every man and of the whole world depend on the sacrifice of Christ."[4] To have come down from the Cross and spared His life would have been to lose the world for which He was dying.

The priests assured the crucified Lord that if He would come down from His cross, they would believe in him. As it had been during His ministry, so it was at the cross—churchmen were invariably asking for signs. Further signs would have been just as spurned as had been the healing of the sick, the exorcising of demons, and the raising of the dead. The Lord did not descend from heaven to perform acts of magic by which the masses would be intrigued. There was only one reason for His coming—He came "to seek and to save that which was lost" (Luke 19:10). That could not be done by gaining the admiration of the priests and losing the adoration of the redeemed.

After more than two thousand years, it is true still that the one reason why people *do believe* in Christ is because He refused to climb down from His cross of redemption. The cross has become a throne from which He rules the world, and the Church is built eternally upon the death of the Son of God. The Christus Rex is a fitting symbol for a crucified and reigning Christ.

Above the head of the Crucified One was nailed the *titulus* that had hung around His neck as the procession followed the cross-bearing King to the scene of execution. The crime of which the accused was charged was always displayed on his body for the purpose of further punishment in the derision and disgust felt by the crowds who lined the roadway to spit at the victim. On the placard around the neck of the Lord were the words, "Jesus, the King of the Jews." It was written in three languages so all would be able to read it, for Jerusalem was full of visitors at Passover time.

The priests disliked the connotation of the *titulus* and sent a delegation to Pilate asking that the words be changed to read, "Jesus, who said He was the King of the Jews." By their own admission, the priests were emphatically clarifying our minds as to whether Jesus had any messianic consciousness. It was obvious to them that He *claimed* to be the King! The governor's refusal to alter what had been written may suggest that he was so sick of the whole thing as to be done with it. Or it may hold overtones of Pilate's uneasy feeling that there was something very special about his victim. Whatever the reason for leaving the titulus untouched, history has verified the wisdom of Pilate in having done so.

John, who was given the responsibility of caring for the mother of Christ, was standing near enough to the dying Savior to hear Him say to Mary, "Look, there is your son," and to John, "And there is your mother" (John 19:26–27 Phillips). Knowing the grief that was nearly destroying His mother and the heartache that was tearing apart the disciple of love, Christ was deeply concerned that they both be cared for and have the comfort of one another's interest. "They needed each other," writes Williams, "if their faith was to blossom into understanding and a new loyalty. Mary needed to lean upon John and John needed someone to draw out the latent forces of his soul."[5]

What a privilege to care for the mother of the Lord, to share the memories of One whom they both loved and worshipped!

Furthermore, it was a source of dying comfort for Jesus to know that Mary was being cared for by the one disciple most capable of understanding her. He must have known that she stood to be the subject of scorn for having been His mother. The Church was eventually to honor her, but no one in Israel, except Jesus' most intimate friends, held her in high regard during her earthly life.

In the midst of all the confusion, the shouting and jeering and cursing, one of the criminals executed with Jesus discovered the redeeming grace of God. "Remember me," he begged of Jesus, "when you have come to your kingdom." Salvation came at the eleventh hour to that dying thief because he did two things: He acknowledged his sin ("We've only got what we deserve"), and he confessed Christ's divine reign for his own life. To believe in Christ as King when the life was oozing from His wounds took more faith than we can begin to comprehend. There was no mistaking the fact that the dying thief knew that the kingdom of God was both present and coming, since he believed in the King as He was dying. In this insight, he recognized the mission of Christ into the world as the Lord Himself conceived it. No one else—not even the disciples—so perfectly understood it. The dying thief believed that Jesus was on His way to a throne.

We are not surprised, in view of this staggering truth about the thief's insight into the accomplished yet anticipated nature of the kingdom, to hear Jesus reply, "This very day you will be with Me in paradise" (Luke 23:43 Phillips). And where is paradise? Since Calvary, the dying Christian no longer enters some dark prison house of waiting, but is admitted directly into the presence of the risen Christ (see the chapter on Saturday of Holy Week). And to be with Him will be paradise, wherever the location of that place may be. Paradise is the restoration of the early state of created humankind in the garden of Eden, when communication between the Lord and His children is once again unbroken by sin. "During earthly life," writes Andrew Blackwood, "we know spiritual birth, infancy, and adolescence. In the life of the world to come we shall know spiritual maturity. That world of spiritual perfection is paradise."[6]

From noon until three o'clock on Friday, heaven hid its face in a mantle of midnight as the Son of God died. Even the sun refused to look at that foul act of deicide. It was ashamed to be a part of the same natural order as rebellious man. The veil which separated the Holy of Holies from the people was ripped apart in the fury of the raging storm. Since that moment, man has been granted access to God through a new Mediator, Christ, by whom we have direct and personal access to the heavenly Father.

The death of Christ paved the way to the throne of God, to the mercy seat, and every seeker after God is now invited to come to the Father through the atoning work of our redeeming Lord. As the high priest had rent his priestly robe when accusing Jesus of blasphemy, so now God rent the robe which wrapped the holy place in the wake of the high priest's blasphemy against the Lord. Never again would God allow a veil of human frailty to restrain man in his penitence from finding the eternal spirit of love and forgiveness. That sacrifice had ended all sacrifices, and God had accepted it as final!

A mark of Jesus' humanity and humiliation is observed in His cry for water. He who was the Water of Life, who offered living water to the woman at Sychar, was now condemned to thirst Himself. But the complete identification of the dying Christ with man's finiteness and sin is most poignantly depicted in His cry of dereliction: "My God, My God, why hast Thou forsaken Me?" To be forsaken by God is to experience hell indeed. To be eternally separated from Him who is the Source of life itself is to suffer the pangs and sorrows of eternal death, to exist in continual death.

It was this horror of having failed in His mission and being divorced from God that Jesus faced on Calvary.

> He is dying in apparent failure; His love is rejected; yet just because that love remains perfect through its rejection it leads Him to feel as His own the horrible sin which prompts that rejection. By the completeness of His sympathy its burden becomes His own, and He experiences that alienation from God which is the obverse of accepted sin.[7]

The reality of hell was endured by the Son of God for me.

Luke records as the final word of Jesus, "Father, into thy hands I commit my spirit!" (23:46), while John recalls hearing the Master cry, "It is finished" (19:30 KJV). We will not go wrong if we insist on both phrases. The two affirmations are theologically similar. The word that John uses is *tetelestai*, and, while "It is finished" is an acceptable translation, it could well be rendered, "It is paid." Archeologists have found this word inscribed on unearthed fragments of potsherd which appear to have been receipts given to citizens for payment of taxes to Rome. In such cases, the idea was that of having paid a debt in full. When one recalls that the early church understood the death of Christ as substitution, it is at once recognized that John probably construed the word that he heard fall from the parched lips of Christ to mean, "I have paid the debt of sin for man." Paul even speaks of our having been "bought with a price" (1 Cor. 6:20 KJV), and Peter declares that we "were not redeemed with corruptible things, as silver and gold ... but with the precious blood of Christ" (1 Peter 1:18–19 KJV).

Squarely in the middle of his excellent little work *The Victor Speaks*, Schlink succinctly summarizes the work of Christ on the cross:

> The Kingdom of God is accomplished, even though the Churches and kingdoms of this world struggle so hard against it. To all of us who think that we are in a stage of transition or even only in the beginning, who are vexed by the little that we accomplish and the great things that we resolve with a holy intention and do not accomplish—also to ... sinners it is said: It is finished! Jesus' work is accomplished, God is glorified on the earth. In fact, so completely is it finished on the cross that nothing, nothing at all, could be added by man.[8]

When Luke's narrative implies the last word to have been a self-committal of Christ to the Father, we are to understand it in the context of the modern expression "Mission accomplished." An English New Testament scholar illustrates this fact with a picture painted during World War I. It portrays a signaler lying dead in no-man's-land, where he had been ordered to repair a broken cable. In the picture, he has completed his task, although he lies cold in death, for in his stiffening hands he is holding together the severed ends of the cable. The caption beneath the picture is only one word: *Through*.[9]

If Jesus thought of His is death as the fulfillment of His work, then this word is much the same in meaning as the payment motif in John. The Lord had won the battle in the garden of Gethsemane, but it was not until the last breath on the cross that the peace treaty was signed! The work that His Father had sent Him to do had been accomplished, and now He was going home! And what a homecoming that must have been as the hosts of heaven welcomed the returning hero who had vanquished heaven's greatest foe!

During the six lonely, painful hours on the cross, Christ had spoken only seven times. Each utterance was brief and simple. At a time when Toyohiko Kagawa was almost blind from working in the slums of Japan, he got out of a sickbed and made an all-night journey to keep a speaking engagement. After the grueling experience that was his in trying to make such a trip in an ill condition, he made a poor appearance in his wrinkled clothes, and his address was short and simple. A young, well-dressed, sophisticated college student from America was very critical of the speaker and his message. In response to his criticism, a friend replied, "A man doesn't have to say much when he is on a cross! Jesus did not need to say much that day on Golgotha. What He did spoke more loudly than what He said."

As the Son of God drew His last breath, the skies began to lighten. It was eerie, as though the elements themselves were trying to adjust to what had happened on the earth. If the Pharisees had wanted a sign, then they had finally gotten it as the light of day returned. The heinous sin that man had committed against God had plunged the earth into darkness, but the love of the Father is really inextinguishable. There is nothing that we can do that will blot out His love forever. It just keeps coming back to break its heart again and again on our adamant spirits.

In keeping with the law, which forbade a body to remain on the cross on the Sabbath, the Jews requested permission of

Pilate to break the legs of the victims, an act which would speed up their death. Often, men lived for days on these crosses before they finally succumbed to death. Not so with Christ. The burden borne by Jesus was that of the human race; therefore, we are amazed that He did not expire sooner!

To ensure Jesus' death, a soldier thrust his spear into the side of the Savior. Blood and water gushed out upon the ground. Apparently, what had happened was that the spear had ruptured the pericardium, the sac around the heart that contains a watery serum, and the blood from the ruptured heart, having mingled with the water, came forth as a clear indication of the nature of His death. Jesus had not died so soon from the nails and the thirst. He had died from *a broken heart*. His great and loving heart had burst under the pressure of the world's sin.

A member of the Sanhedrin named Joseph asked permission to remove the body from the cross. Nicodemus, also a member of the council, came with spices and helped his colleague anoint the body, wrap it in grave linen, and place it in the sepulchre. More than likely, these two men became disciples of the Lord that Friday afternoon as they tenderly prepared His earthly house for its burial. Near to the cross, there was a garden with a virgin tomb, probably the property of Joseph, in which they laid the Master. A huge stone was rolled across the entrance. While the weeping women, including Mary of Magdala, watched the proceedings, the shades of night fell across the sad and sorrowing fellowship of sufferers.

Matthew informs us that the priests and Pharisees requested the governor to place a guard at the tomb and seal its entrance, lest the disciples steal the corpse and say that Christ had risen. The request having been granted, the churchmen took the soldiers and supervised the sealing of the sepulchre to their own satisfaction that such a scheme would be impossible. At last, the Pharisees were rid of their despised enemy. It had been a long, hard fight, but they had won. Nothing could happen now to reverse the finality of the cross. They had shut off the disciples from their Master by a sealed door and a Roman guard. Where they made their mistake, however, was in not sealing the *interior* of the door. But, then, no one had the least thought that anything might happen from *inside* that tomb!

SATURDAY

> And there are also many other things which Jesus did, the which, if they should be written every one, I suppose that even the world itself could not contain the books that should be written. (John 21:25 KJV)[1]

The Day of Retroactive Atonement

The usual studies of the events that transpired during our Lord's final week seem to be totally oblivious to the significance of the seventh day. While it is true that the gospel narratives imply that nothing took place on Saturday of Holy Week, it is quite likely that the Jewish Sabbath may have been the crucified Christ's "busiest" day. After all, had He not been condemned often for "doing good on the Sabbath"? Is there any reason to assume that physical death terminated such deeds of compassion on the first Sabbath of the new age?

The diaphanous sheath of grief that clouded the sight of the Lord's friends, coupled with their unwillingness to even guess at what happens beyond the impenetrable veil of death, made it improbable that so nebulous a matter would be included in eyewitness accounts written by simple men possessed with the reality of what they had seen. While much of what was actually happening in the realm of the Divine Spirit remained translucent or completely unrecognized, there were at least clearly discernible movements and responses of the human Christ on every day—that is, every day except Saturday.

The motionless body of Jesus had been tenderly laid in a tomb before sundown on Friday and remained unseen until sometime during the predawn hours of the eighth day. It is true that no one had access to the sepulchre, but neither would anyone have even faintly entertained the thought that Christ could have been anywhere other than in the grave or engaged in any other endeavor than that which befits the dead. The Master was dead, cold, and lifeless, and the day was a historical blank.

No one knows exactly when Christ rose from the dead. The discovery was made "as it began to dawn," but it is impossible to say whether He rose at five o'clock, two thirty, or twelve fifteen in the morning on that glorious Sunday. The prophecies and the words of the Lord Himself had said only that He would arise on "the third day." But what of His Spirit released at the moment of physical death? Was He not about His Father's business long before first seen by Mary on Sunday morning? Was He not engaged already in the completion of the mission of God, which did not end at His death? Did the Lord, in spirit, return to His unfinished task? The Scriptures reveal that in the interim He made His exit into realms hitherto unvisited by any other than pure spirit. It was the manifestation in physical form that remained to be revealed on the third day.

"Where was Jesus," asks DuBose, "between the moment when His spirit left His body and the moment of His resurrection?

He was certainly not in the tomb. And when Mary found Him in Joseph's garden, near the open sepulchre, He told her that He had not yet ascended to the Father. Where ... then had He been, and what had He been doing?"[2] Were it not for Simon Peter, we might never have known the answer to DuBose's question. Though Peter apparently did not mention it to Mark when he was providing information for the latter's gospel, he does give us more than a clue in the first epistle to bear his own name.

> Christ also died for our sins once and for all. He, the just, suffered for the unjust, to bring us to God. In the body he was put to death; in the spirit he was brought to life. And in the spirit he went and made his proclamation to the imprisoned spirits. They had refused obedience long ago, while God waited patiently in the days of Noah and the building of the ark, and in the ark a few persons, eight in all, were brought to safety through the water. (1 Pet. 3:18–20)

How did Peter know this? One must not forget that Simon was one of the "inner three," the most closely associated and trusted of Jesus' disciples. The Lord appeared to His men on several occasions that are recorded in the Bible. We would be in error to assume that the Lord did not meet with the Eleven at other times, as well. At any of the appearances subsequent to the resurrection, a clarification of the happenings on the Saturday of entombment might have been made. It is quite possible, however, that the secret could have been shared with Simon alone, since to him had been given the highest vote of confidence, the keys of the kingdom (Matt. 16:19), and the special charge to feed the flock (John 21:15-17). When we note that Simon is the only one who makes the statement about the Lord's activity on that particular day, the finger points clearly to this conjecture.

If it is disturbing that Peter did not have Mark mention this secret, then the reason may be that Mark was mainly concerned with writing a short, basic story of the events in the life of the Master, which could be corroborated readily by many witnesses. After the kernel of truth had been well established and verified, others, like Peter, could present the underlying theological and christological secrets revealed to them. The fact that there is no long argument on so significant a theological matter in the writings of Paul would also suggest that the events of Saturday of Holy Week were well-known within the Church.

Among the early fathers of the Church, however, there were varied views. Clement of Alexandria, for example, believed that Christ proclaimed redemption to the saintly Hebrews who had died before His advent, and also to the pagans who had walked in all the light that they had received. The Orthodox Church never accepted his explanation. The more rational interpretation, at least to the mainstream of the early church, was shared by men like Irenaeus, who believed that the Lord released the Old Testament prophets and patriarchs from the prison house of death, where they had been awaiting the final solution to personal salvation from sin in Jesus Christ. Tertullian and Justin Martyr agreed with Irenaeus.

In seeking light on the Petrine passage, some have agreed that Jesus went down into *Hades*, but that the descent had no particular significance that was peculiar to Christ. "He descended into hades" merely means the same as the phrase "crucified, dead, and buried." The note about "preaching" is either ignored or explained away. If this is to be accepted as a valid interpretation, then we still have on our hands the question as to where the living Spirit of Jesus was while people waited for His reappearance. If the Incarnation means that He lived before birth and the resurrection that He lived after death, then it is only logical to argue that such a One also lived in a unique dimension between the crucifixion and Easter Sunday.

Paul believed that Jesus was in *Hades* during the interval that spanned Friday night, Saturday, and part of Saturday night. "Do not say to yourself," he writes, "'Who can go up to heaven?' (that is to bring Christ down), or, 'Who can go down to the abyss?' (to bring Christ up from the dead)" (Rom. 10:6–7). But he did not think of the Savior as being merely in the abode of departed spirits, as one of the immobile dead. The apostle quotes from a psalm as he writes to the Ephesians of Christ's exaltation: "He ascended into the heights with captives in his train; He gave gifts to men." (Then, he adds, for clarification, "Now, the word 'ascended' implies that he also descended to the lowest level, down to the very earth. He who descended is no other than he who ascended far above all heavens, so that he might fill the universe" [Eph. 4:8–10]). The comment made by Paul makes it clear that he thought of Jesus as being in *Hades*, and the quotation "with captives in his train" may suggest the same truth as found in the Petrine passage. When the apostle writes to the Philippians, he emphatically affirms that "at the name of Jesus every knee should bow, in heaven and on earth and under the earth" (2:9 RSV). The latter expression seems to have some definite relationship in Paul's mind with the work of the Redeemer in *Hades*.

Jesus' statement, recorded by John, "I am the way; I am the truth and I am life; no one comes to the Father except by me" (14:6), has been the subject of some controversy. Weatherhead, for instance, says of this passage, "I do not believe that Jesus ever said, 'No one cometh unto the Father but by me.' ... Are all the great saints of the Old Testament, and indeed, the great saints and seers of other religions, excluded from the presence of the Father because they had never heard of Jesus Christ? The supposition is ridiculous."[3] But who is to deny the words of Holy Writ and accept the statement of any exegete who thus weakens the unique deliverance from sin and access to God provided by Jesus? It is strongly suggested that those Old Testament saints and seers of other religions *have* had or *will* have their confrontation with the Lord in *Hades*.

God is not a capricious executioner who destroys human beings without giving them a chance. Those who lived in what light they had prior to the coming of Christ were privileged to hear the gospel preached and to respond to it in the realm of the dead. Lockyer suggests,

> When Peter refers to Christ as going to preach to the spirits in prison, he may have referred to His ministry during His absence from the earth as His body lay in the tomb. To the righteous in "Abraham's bosom" He would proclaim the message of deliverance when at His ascension He would take them all to be with Himself.[4]

Righteous persons who live today without advantage of hearing about Christ may be given that opportunity in some divine rendezvous prepared by the Lord Himself, possibly in Hades. People still find God through the Lord Jesus Christ, and there is no other path made plain to us. The inimitable Denny wrote,

The Christian faith is a specific form of dependence on God, and to cavil at the atonement is to begin the process of gradually abandoning that sense of dependence. It is to refuse to allow it to be conditioned by Christ at the central and vital point, the point at which the sinner is reconciled to God; and if we can do without Christ there, we can do without Him altogether.[5]

To assume that there is some cosmic "Christ" in all world religions is an untenable theory and must not be confused with the moral law written within human flesh.

"We will be wise," says Barclay, "to take the Peter passage in its obvious sense. Peter meant it to mean that Jesus preached to the shades of men in the world of the dead."[6] And what was the content of that message that He preached? It was the "kerygma" of the early church, which would later be proclaimed by Paul and the apostles. Invariably, the proclamation of the New Testament heralds of the gospel was summed up in three points: (1) Christ is the fulfillment of the prophecies concerning the coming Messiah; (2) He has been put to death for our redemption, and God has raised Him from the dead as an assurance of man's eternal life; and, therefore, (3) let all repent and believe the gospel of salvation.

History records some magnificent preaching experiences. The preaching of Noah before the flood, that of Ezekiel to the stubborn Israelites, John the Baptist to the "generation of vipers," Christ on the shores of Galilee, Peter at Pentecost, Paul on Mars' Hill, Chrysostom before the empress at Constantinople, Savonarola in Florence, and Wesley to the grime-covered miners of England are examples of the proclamation of the divine message. But what of this preaching, this pulpit, and this congregation as Christ spoke to the departed spirits? It is exciting to imagine with what joy that message, preached the first time by Christ Himself in the abode of the dead, must have been received! What had seemed like an eternity to the imprisoned righteous of the ages, who were waiting for the day of their emancipation, was finally over.

In light of the biblical revelation of Christ and His redemptive act, it would seem that Clement may have been more nearly correct than the early church was willing to concede. With his broad vision and magnanimous spirit, he seemed to catch the inclusive love of God, which reaches out to all people who accept the light that has been given to them. While Clement would not have dared to suggest that the pagans could find eternal life without Christ, he would never think of confining the preaching of the Savior in Hades only to the faithful in Israel or to the disobedient who lived prior to the flood.

This is not to suggest that there will be a *second chance* for valid repentance in the next world. What we are saying is that this passage in Peter's epistle hints at what must be true if God is the loving Father we say He is—that is, that every person will be assured at least *one* chance to confront the redeeming Lord. We need not fear for the state of people who die without having heard the gospel. God, in His mighty love, will find His own way to allow every soul the choice to become a son of God and joint heir with Jesus Christ.

This, then, is what our Lord was doing while people thought of Him as being stretched on a slab of gray limestone in the grip of death. He was still about the Father's business, *still* doing good to the oppressed, and preaching deliverance to the captives!

While the friends of Christ grieved in bleak despair, the Son of God, behind the stage on which men were playing their little game, was engaged in a full and final renovation of the realm of the dead! At the very moment when His enemies were strutting with pride over the annihilation of Jesus of Nazareth, the Lord was quietly conquering the forces of evil that had nailed Him to the cross. Death was forever dead, and Satan, though permitted to continue the pursuit of his ugly cause, was divested of all his lethal weapons and rendered incapable of final victory.

Saturday was "moving day" for pre-Calvary men and women who had waited for a chance to respond to the call of Christ. What a sight that souls on the other side must have witnessed as, led by the penitent thief, the first man to bypass Hades, multitudes of redeemed and glorified saints walked from their concentration camp into the sunlit freedom of God's heavenly world! The dark night was over and the day of resurrection had dawned. Many hours before Mary was to look upon that glorified image of her Lord, the realm of the dead had been evangelized with the gospel of redemption.

SUNDAY

Why are you looking among the dead for one who is alive? He is not here; he has risen. (Luke.4:5–6 TEV)[1]

The Day When Death Died

If Jesus were dead by three o'clock Friday afternoon, and the accounts seem to indicate that He was, then we can imagine how rushed Joseph and Nicodemus were in getting the body off the cross and into the sepulchre. Jewish law was quite specific, stipulating that a crucified victim must be interred before the beginning of the Sabbath, or sundown on Friday. With a maximum of three hours in which to get permission from Pilate, remove the Lord's body, wash and wrap it, and deposit the remains inside a burial chamber, the two distinguished friends were forced to move with clockwork precision. No doubt they had commandeered the help of some assistants. There was no time to waste on any customary preburial chores. The important thing was complying with the law, lest the authorities take the body of Jesus by force and bury it in shame in the potter's field.

As the first hint of dawn softly fell across the slumbering city of Jerusalem that Sunday morning, Mary of Magdala and several other grieving women approached the gate of the garden wherein the Master had been buried. They had come for the express purpose of completing the anointing and preparation of the deceased for His permanent entombment. Having done their work well but in great haste, Joseph and Nicodemus had probably agreed for the women to put the final touches of tender care on the body, in compliance with Hebrew tradition, as soon as the Sabbath was past. Thus, Mary lost no time in getting to the sepulchre as early as the law permitted.

Whether they knew of Pilate's sealing of the tomb and the detachment of soldiers who had stood guard through the night is uncertain. What seemed to concern them as they came in sight of the garden was the matter of gaining entrance into a sepulchre across the opening of which had been rolled a stone of ponderous size, which they knew they themselves could not move. One wonders why they had not made arrangements to have several of Jesus' friends meet them for this purpose. It is quite possible that the Eleven may have been afraid to show themselves anywhere near the grave, for fear of being arrested. On the other hand, it is possible that the women may have known about the presence of the guards and hoped that they would help them move the stone. The nearer they came to their destination, the more nervous they grew in anticipation of confronting the Roman soldiers and their possible refusal to assist them with their plans.

In the shadows of the early morning, the women were unable to see anything distinctly. Their uneasiness mounted as they followed the path through the olive trees, not because of the sound of armed men, but because there were no sounds at all. The quietness would have seemed to imply that there was no one near the tomb. Suddenly, Matthew records, the earth beneath their feet began to tremble as an unearthly light commenced to play around the entrance to the sepulchre. As they stood, holding to a gnarled olive branch for support, a figure in white appeared and rolled away the stone. From within the open burial chamber, a blinding light came flooding into the garden. The "keepers" were paralyzed with fright.

Some have argued that the unidentified spokesman in the garden was a young man who had been left to tell the story. Indeed, Mark and Luke are ambiguous as to the real nature of the messenger, but Matthew and John both emphatically claim that the spokesman was an angelic being or possibly two such heavenly messengers. The testimony of John holds a great deal of weight since, though his narrative was written quite late, he was an eyewitness! If the personage at the sepulchre was a human being and nothing more, the door is left open for all kinds of strange and twisted explanations. Some have even suggested that a group of men had been to the tomb earlier that morning and rolled away the stone, leaving a sentry to explain what had happened.

Now, it must be noted that the stone had not been rolled away so that Jesus could get out. The resurrection had already transpired, and the risen Lord had emerged from the sepulchre as He was later to enter the upper room, without the necessity of an open door. Space and time were to be meaningless to the eternal spirit who was no longer restricted by earthly laws of a material and interim cosmos. Before the stone was removed, the Lord was abroad in His kingdom.

There was only one reason for the appearance of the angels and the dramatic opening of the sepulcher—evidence that the tomb was empty and had been *evacuated before the door was opened.* The stone was moved, then, not to let Jesus *out,* but to let the world *in* on the divine secret! Christ was alive in a new and glorious way—He was now living in a dimension where earthly limits on existence and being were completely impotent. Some still argue that the empty tomb proves nothing. To us who believe, however, next to the continuing personal experience with the living Lord, it is the one grand clincher for the fact of the resurrection.

Matthew speaks of an angel sitting on the stone (28:2); Mark, of a "young man sitting on the right side clothed in a long white garment" (16:5 KJV); Luke, of "two men ... in dazzling light" (24:4 Phillips); and John, of "two angels in white sitting where the body of Jesus had lain" (20:12 RSV). Apparently, there were more heavenly troops on the scene of victory that morning than is normally considered. Maybe the whole "twelve legions of angels" Jesus had talked about earlier had poured into that little garden!

No one should find the variations in the accounts to be cause for unbelief. It is the fact that there is such variety in the reporting that convinces the reader that there has been no attempt at collusion on the part of the reporters. "If the Gospels were put together by fabricators, why did they not see to it that their lies were in harmony? These differences in the narratives show sincerity and independence on the part of the narrators."[2] Each narrator is reporting only what impressed him, or the eyewitness who imparted the information used by the narrator, on the occasion of the effulgence of divine glory in that Middle Eastern garden.

To the women, whose hearts were wildly pounding within their breasts, the angel calmly said, "Do not be so fearful. There is no need for alarm. Jesus of Nazareth, who was crucified, is no longer here. He is risen!" Then, rising from his position and beckoning with his hand, the divine messenger reassuringly added, "Come and see for yourself. Here is where they laid Him, but He is no longer here" (Matt. 28:5-6, author's paraphrase).

What they saw was enough to make them pale with fear and wonder! John is the one who gives a detailed description of what their eyes beheld. According to the beloved disciple, the women had fled from the garden to report to the Eleven what they had seen. And it was when Peter and John arrived at the tomb that the earthshaking, history-making news conquered their hearts. There, before their eyes, was unmistakable evidence that Jesus was alive.

What they saw were the grave-cloths in which Jesus had been interred. John describes the scene with exciting vividness: Peter "saw the linen cloths lying there and the cloth which had been around Jesus' head. It was not lying with the linen cloths but was rolled up by itself" (20:6–7 TEV). Obviously, the linen shroud that had encased the body lay still on the rocky ledge, collapsed under the weight of Nicodemus' "hundred pounds of spices," but retaining somewhat the outline of the human form of Jesus. The napkin, or turban-like head bandage, was folded and left lying apart from the shroud. Everything was just as Jesus had left it when He walked out of His crypt and into the night air. Nothing was disturbed, nothing at all. The grave-cloths were silent witnesses to the literal resurrection of the Lord.

When John explains that he joined the wide-eyed Simon Peter inside the tomb, he adds that he also "saw and believed." It is clear to all that the source of his being convinced of the resurrection lay not in the empty tomb, but in the indisputable evidence provided by the linens. "John was convinced," observes a modern lawyer, "not at all by visions or voices or embodied expectations of his own, but in the most matter-of-fact way and by the very same kind of observation that we ourselves use and rely upon in the common affairs of life."³

There was no plausible explanation for the orderly appearance of the sepulchre except the fact that Christ had risen of His own divine power. No one could look at the cloths and argue with any credibility that the body of Jesus had been removed by human hands. If so, why would intruders have taken the time to unwrap the corpse when such an act of tomb robbing would have been carried out in a hurry, lest they be detected? "Disorder and disarray are the earmarks of a prowling visitor."⁴ How would such outsiders have gotten into the sepulchre and out again with a dead body without being attacked by the guards? And what is even more convincing, how could anyone have removed the linens and turban without disturbing the shape of the body, which was visibly evident? There was absolutely no room for debate. What had happened had been initiated from *inside* the sealed doorway and from *inside* the linen swathes! The most glorious spot on earth had become, of all places, the interior of a grave!

The first two narratives mention the early appearance of the risen Christ to Mary of Magdala, but it is the fourth gospel that tells us precisely what happened. Mary had been weeping when the angel sought to clear up the mystery of the vacant sepulchre. Having heard the angel's confusing words, Mary turned, probably on a stunned impulse, to leave the garden. Hardly had she moved from the doorway when she was confronted by one whom Mary thought to be the keeper of the garden. The question He asked, "Why are you weeping?" would have been a strange inquiry under normal conditions to make of anyone crying at a grave. But on this occasion, the question was perfectly in order. There was not the least reason for tears—only for rejoicing!

Trying to talk between her sobs, Mary pleaded with the "gardener" to tell her where the body of Jesus had been taken, in order that she might give it proper anointing and burial. It is quite likely that she had not so much as lifted her eyes from the ground while she spoke. If she had raised her eyes, they were so filled with tears that it was impossible to focus them on the face of the one with whom she conversed. At any rate, Mary did not recognize the "stranger" until He called her name. Often, she had heard her name spoken in shame until the Lord had forgiven and redeemed her. Jesus was the first man she had ever met who uttered her name in honest kindness. Thus, when He called her "Mary," she caught her breath! It was the Master.

Spontaneously, as though it were the natural thing to do, Mary threw herself at the pierced feet of her Redeemer. "Do not touch Me," warned Jesus, "for as yet I have not ascended to My Father. Rather, go and tell My friends where I have gone." And, if we bring all the narratives together at this point, Abbott is probably right in arguing that the confusing word about meeting the disciples in Galilee is better understood as a reference to the ascension by which Christ was going away to "prepare a place" for His own.[5]

If this is the case, then Jesus was to ascend into the abode of the Father, where He would intercede before the "mercy seat" for the disciples, sometime between Sunday morning and that evening. "Consequently, the Ascension, which will in some sense complete the Resurrection, effects a new relationship between the disciples and the Father ... The triumphant Redeemer will ever make intercession for His own. They will have access to the Father through Him."[6] This is closely akin to Barth's belief that, as the Incarnation put God in man's place, so the ascension puts man in God's place. Thus, the reconciliation between God and man is completed.[7]

According to Luke (24:39), Jesus appeared in the upper room that very night and welcomed the "touch" of His men. The ascension had been effected. There is no reason to be unduly distressed about the references in the book of Acts (1:1–11) to the "forty days" that elapsed between the resurrection and the ascension. Luke wrote of both ascensions, and it is no contradiction to assume that there may have been two (or even more) ascensions in view of the fact that the glorified Lord was fully at home in either world and, therefore, unbound by the natural barriers known to man.

One of the most intriguing facets of the account of the resurrection is that the narrators are perfectly honest in their admission that the disciples did not expect the event that had happened and bluntly refused to believe the "delirious reports" until they had seen for themselves. The Church has been unjustly hard on Thomas because of his honest doubt. What he demanded by way of proof was no more than that demanded by the other ten. Not one of the disciples believed until he had seen the Lord. Thus, when Jesus said to Thomas, "You are to be congratulated on believing what you have seen, but those who will later believe without seeing have the highest accolade of all," He was speaking to all His followers and not just to he who was receiving the brunt of His words.

When the evidence was in, there was not the faintest trace of a doubt among the excited disciples. Christ was alive! It was not something that they had heard from Mary or Peter. They had seen for themselves, and never again could they keep quiet about what they had witnessed. As soon as the two unnamed followers, traveling to Emmaus on the afternoon of the day of the resurrection, had walked and talked with the Master and watched Him break bread before them, they ran the full seven miles back to Jerusalem to tell the Eleven what they had experienced. Mary had already told Peter and John, and soon every eyewitness of the living Lord was in the streets of the city telling the unbelievable story.

Since the nineteenth century, numerous efforts have been made toward weakening the biblical account of the literal resurrection of Christ and the fact of the empty tomb. Some have speculated that Jesus had a substitute, possibly Simon of Cyrene, and that He slipped away from the soldiers unnoticed. Others, like Venturini, have claimed that the Lord was removed from the cross in a swoon and revived in the cool sepulchre. Of course, the oldest attempt at falsifying the report was made by the Jews themselves, who bribed the soldiers on guard at the tomb to say that the disciples stole the body while they slept.

Scholars like Strauss[8] and Renan[9] argue that Mary and the disciples only *thought* that they saw the Master, that grief born of love generated the appearances, which were really only subjective visions. Keim[10] insists that the resurrection was a purely spiritual event but that the visions were not conjured up by man's imagination. They were, rather, "telegrams from heaven," visions induced by God Himself. Lake[11] suggests that the women arrived in the garden at the wrong tomb and were frightened away by a man who sought to guide them to the place of Jesus' burial. Though he did not disbelieve in the survival of man's life, Lake did not accept the resurrection of the material body and, therefore, refused the authenticity of the biblical record of an empty tomb as having any bearing on the events of that first Easter.

A contemporary writer shares this preference for a purely spiritual resurrection. "We should redefine the word 'resurrection'; it should mean for us, not what the word originally meant—a resurrection of a physical body, but what it meant in part for the Apostle Paul, a rising again of all that is vital in one's nature, the essential personality."[12]

But all these are merely the rationalizations of men who do not want to accept the report of the New Testament eyewitnesses. They cast doubt on either their intelligence or their reliability. It is still wiser to rely on the witness of those who have seen something firsthand than to trust theoretical notions, regardless of how logical they may appear.

It is difficult to comprehend how men recognized as intelligent can question the power of the Almighty, the ways of the eternal, the wisdom of God. The resurrection of Jesus Christ is the one fact of history best established by cumulative evidence. Yet it is regularly questioned by men of scholarly bent as though it were a mark of intelligence to be agnostic in areas where God is believed to have acted! "If the evidence is pointing us towards a resurrection of an utterly unique sort," writes Ramsey, "we will not be incredulous, for the Christ is Himself a unique and transcendent fact in history."[13]

The Church of Jesus Christ is built on the resurrection. Incarnation, ministry, atonement, resurrection, ascension, and *parousia* (second coming) are all mighty acts in the eternal plan of divine redemption. And while it is presumptuous to say what God could or could not do, it is in keeping with the heart and core of the New Testament to affirm that man's deliverance from the bondage of sin would not be complete without any one of these great events. If there can be any one of these events in the life of Christ and the long stream of historical progression that can be considered as the pivot around which all else turns, that single event would undoubtedly be the resurrection. But the splendor that increased in volume through those eight days of glory, from the triumphal entry to the empty tomb, has still not reached its zenith. We have yet to see the fullest and grandest glory of all when He shall come in mighty power to reign as Lord of Lords and King of Kings.

All that has happened in Christ is an earnest of what is yet to be. The kingdom, which dawned in His person, will be consummated at the end of the age. Life eternal, which has already begun with the thrilling foretaste of meaningful existence in a risen Lord, must be perfected in the full bloom of eschatological reality. The Christian's experience in the Holy Spirit has only commenced to grow as our awareness of the inexhaustible present tense of God leads us deeper and farther along the path of spiritual communion toward that far-distant day when "we shall see Him as He is!" (1 John 3:2).

ENDNOTES

Sunday: A Welcome That Made God Cry

1   Cf. Matt. 21:1–11; Mark 11:1–11; Luke 19:28–46; John 12:12–19.
2   Edwin McNeill Poteat, *The Scandal of the Cross* (New York: Harper and Bros., 1928), 132.
3   William Temple, *Palm Sunday to Easter* (London: SCM Press, 1942), 10.
4   Ethelbert Stauffer, *Jesus and His Story* (New York: Alfred Knopf, Inc., 1960), 111.
5   Alfred Edersheim, *The Life and Times of Jesus the Messiah* (Grand Rapids, MI: Eerdmans Publishing Co., 1967), ii, 373.

Monday: A Religion that Made God Angry

1   Cf. Matt. 21:12–19; Mark 11:12–17; Luke 19:45–46.
2   F. W. Farrar, *The Life of Christ* (New York: World Publishing Co., 1913), 318.
3   Edward A. McDowell, *Jesus and His Cross* (Nashville: Broadman Press, 1944), 165.
4   Not to suggest a *replacement* but a *postponement* of the nation of Israel.
5   Raymond E. Brown, *The Anchor Bible* (New York: Doubleday, 1966), xxix, 122.
6   Eldersheim, op. cit., 375.

Tuesday: The Day that Made God Tired

1. Cf. Matt. 21:23–26:2; Mark 11:20–13:37; Luke 20:1–21:38.
2. Walter E. Bundy, *The Passion Week* (Chicago: Willett, Clark and Colby, 1930).
3. H. P. Liddon, *The Divinity of Our Lord and Savior Jesus Christ* (London: Rivingtons, 1889), 181, 185.
4. Gunther Bornkamm, *Jesus of Nazareth* (New York: Harper and Row, 1960), 172.
5. J. Gresham Machen, *The Virgin Birth* (Grand Rapids, MI: Baker Book House, 1930, reprint), 129.
6. C. S. Lewis, *Letters to an American Lady* (Grand Rapids, MI: Eerdmans Publishing Co., 1967), 38.
7. Fulton J. Sheen, *Life of Christ* (New York: McGraw-Hill Publishing Co., 1958), 288.
8. Helmut Thielicke, *The Waiting Father* (New York: Harper and Row, 1959), 186.
9. George A. Buttrick, *The Parables of Jesus* (New York: Harper and Bros., 1928), 230.

Wednesday: And God Rested

1. Cf. Matt. 26:3–16; Mark 14:1–11; Luke 22:1–6.
2. Hugh J. Schonfield. *The Passover Plot* (London: Hutchinson, 1965).
3. James S. Kirtley, *His Last Thursday* (Philadelphia: Judson Press, 1934), 31–32.
4. F. W. Krummacher, *The Suffering Savior* (Chicago: Moody Press, 1947), 13.
5. George A. Sweazy, *Effective Evangelism* (New York: Harper and Bros., 1953), 34.
6. William Barclay, *The Mind of Jesus* (New York: Harper and Row, 1960), 197.
7. Edersheim, op. cit., 478.

Thursday: The Day of Suffering Fellowship

1. Cf. Matt. 26:17–30; Mark 14:12–26; Luke 22:7–38; John 13:1–17:26.
2. Barclay, op. cit., 215.
3. James S. Stewart, *The Life and Teaching of Jesus Christ* (Nashville: Abingdon Press, 1958).
4. Stauffer, op. cit., 113–114.
5. S. Pearce Carey, *Jesus and Judas* (London: Hodder and Stoughton, 1931), 114.
6. Andrew Murray, *Like Christ* (New York: Grosset and Dunlap, n.d.), 16–17.
7. Ibid., 29.
8. Jean Danielou, *Primitive Christian Symbols* (Baltimore: Helicon Press, 1961), 145.

Thursday: The Night of Divine Sadness

1. Cf. Matt. 26:31–56; Mark 14:27–52; Luke 22:39–53; John 18:1–12.
2. Herbert Lockyer, *The Week that Changed the World* (Grand Rapids, MI: Zondervan Publishing House, 1968), 54–55.
3. Claren E. Macartney, *Twelve Great Questions about Christ* (Grand Rapids, MI: Baker Book House, 1956), 110.
4. James C. McRuer, *The Trial of Jesus* (Toronto: Clarke, Irwin, and Co., 1964), 3.
5. Carey, op. cit., 14.
6. David Redding, *The Miracles of Christ* (Old Tappan, NJ: Fleming H. Revell Co., 1964), 105.

Thursday: The Night When the Priests Defied God

1. Cf. Matt. 26:57–76; Mark 14:53–72; Luke 22:54–71; John 18:13–27.
2. A. P. Stout, *Trials and Crucifixion of Christ* (Cincinnati: Standard Publishing Co., 1886), 9.
3. Krummacher, op. cit., 166.
4. Karl Heim, *Jesus the World's Perfecter* (Philadelphia: Muhlenberg Press, 1961), 189.

5   C. F. Chase, *The Trial of Jesus Christ* (London: Simpkin, Marshall and Co., 1876), 78.
6   C. H. Mayo, "St. Peter's Token of the Cock Crow," *Journal of Theological Studies* 22, no. 88 (July 1921): 367.

Friday: The Morning When the State Deserted God

1   Cf. Matt. 27:1–32; Mark 15:1–21; Luke 23:1–31; John 18:28–19:16.
2   John Watson, *The Upper Room* (New York: Dodd, Mead and Co., 1895), 51.
3   William Shakespeare, *Macbeth*, act 5, scene 1.

Friday: Mission Accomplished

1   Cf. Matt. 27:33–66; Mark 15:22–47; Luke 23:32–56a; John 19:17–42.
2   William Cannon, *The Redeemer* (Nashville: Abingdon Press, 1961), 162.
3   David Smith, *The Days of His Flesh* (New York: George H. Doran Co., 1905), 495.
4   Markus Barth, *Was Christ's Death a Sacrifice?* (Edinburgh: Oliver and Boyd Ltd., 1961), 55.
5   Clayton Williams, *The Dark Road to Triumph* (New York: Thomas Y. Crowell, 1960), 55–56.
6   Andrew Blackwood, *The Voice from the Cross* (Grand Rapids, MI: Baker Book House, 1955), 25.
7   Temple, op. cit., 28.
8   Edmund Schlink, *The Victor Speaks* (St. Louis: Concordia Publishing House, 1958), 48.
9   A. M. Hunter, *Teaching and Preaching the New Testament* (Philadelphia: Westminster Press, 1963), 104.

Saturday: The Day of Retroactive Atonement

1   Cf. Luke 23:56b; Eph. 4:9–10; Phil. 2:9; 1 Pet. 3:18–20.
2   Henry Wade DuBose, *We Believe* (Richmond, VA: John Knox Press, 1946), 46.

3. Leslie Weatherhead, *The Christian Agnostic* (Nashville: Abingdon-Cokesbury Press, 1965), 66.
4. Lockyer, op. cit., 103.
5. James Denney, *The Death of Christ* (London: Tyndale House, 1951), 40.
6. William Barclay, *The Apostle's Creed for Everyman* (New York: Harper and Row, 1967), 126.

Sunday: The Day When Death Died

1. Cf. Matt. 28:1–20; Mark 16:1–20; Luke 24:1–49; John 20:1–21:25.
2. Macartney, op. cit., 124.
3. Albert L. Roper, *Did Jesus Rise from the Dead?* (Grand Rapids, MI: Zondervan Publishing House, 1965), 48.
4. Ibid., 37.
5. Edwin A. Abbott, *Paradosis* (London: Adam and Charles Black Ltd., 1904), 200.
6. Yarnold, op. cit., 30.
7. Karl Barth, *Dogmatics in Outline* (Zurich: Evangelischer Verlag, 1949), 115.
8. David F. Strauss, *The Life of Jesus* (New York: Blanchard, 1855).
9. Ernest Renan, *The Life of Christ* (New York: World Publishing Co., 1941).
10. Theodore Keim, *History of Jesus of Nazareth* (London: Williams and Norgate Ltd., 1873), 83.
11. Kirsopp Lake, *The Historical Evidence for the Resurrection of Jesus Christ* (New York: G. P. Putnam's Sons, 1907).
12. A. J. Ebbutt, *Who Do You Say that I Am?* (Philadelphia: Westminster Press, 1957), 127.
13. Michael Ramsey, *The Resurrection of Christ* (London: Geoffrey Bles, 1945), 56.

Printed in the USA
CPSIA information can be obtained
at www.ICGtesting.com
CBHW031057051223
2167CB00002BA/8